i

Dedication

This book is based upon lessons learned from successes, failures, mentors who cared, and taskmasters who wouldn't let me "just get by." It would make sense that I would dedicate this book to all of those involved in my journey, for they are why I am writing this book today. I am deeply grateful to them all. But this book is much more than those experiences and great relationships, so my dedication couldn't go to them.

This book is dedicated wholly, and solely, to my wife, Maggie. Without Maggie, this book would be a story of a life that coexists with the void that can only be filled by your soulmate.

Maggie, my soulmate, this book is dedicated to you.

VELOCITY
LEADERSHIP

Leading with
PURPOSE, IMPACT & ACHIEVEMENT

TRIBUTE
PUBLISHING
2017

"Join me in eradicating weak leadership by being a bold, VELOCITY LEADER."

- Kelly Castor

Contents

Introduction

ve·loc·i·ty: Direction *plus* speed *minus* drag = Velocity

Looking back, it's clear that my entire life experience has been preparing me for what I do as my vocation. In fact, it's more than a vocation. It's who I am. I've been a student of human behavior, cause and effect, for as long as I can remember. I've always been fascinated with how people attempt to motivate others, develop them, coach them, whatever term you want to use. Over the years, I've been led and managed by people who were great at it and people who weren't. If you are reading this book, you can probably say the same thing.

In 2002, I decided to focus on leadership and management development full-time and launched my company, Velocity Leadership. After various levels of responsibility ranging from a territory sales rep to the C-suite to owning my own company, I was convinced there was a substantial need for management and leadership training. I had no idea how big the need really was.

Fast-forward to today, and my company mission has transformed into a bold movement. That movement is to "eradicate weak leadership." Not just improve it. Eradicate it. To do something so large, so significant, requires boldness. It requires us to be Bold Leaders.

Unfortunately, much of what we have been told and taught about leadership is either missing a key ingredient, or the ingredients are being developed in the wrong order.

When it comes to the development of a highly effective leader, syntax is important, extremely important.

As you'll learn in the subsequent pages, this order is one of the important drivers as to why I wrote this book in the first place. As leaders, we are not challenging ourselves to address the necessary components in the right order to ensure that we are part of the eradication of weak leadership instead of its perpetuation.

Additionally, if we are getting the components in the right order, we need to be bold in applying those learnings to ensure that we aren't doing the hard work of syntax and still being mediocre in our effectiveness. It's the classic learning versus doing. We need to learn, then boldly do. This is how we not only eradicate weak leadership, but also increase high-performance leadership.

Velocity Leadership is both my company and a development process. It requires the fuel of boldness in its application. You'll see Bold Leadership intertwined with Velocity Leadership throughout this book. This is to ensure that we realize the emphasis and discipline we need to apply the tools and understandings in a manner that has a meaningful and sustainable impact with those we lead and work with.

As you read this book, I challenge you to "look in the mirror" first. It's easy to read some of the examples of weak leadership and think of others that you've known in the past. Use this as a trigger to STOP and ask yourself, "Do I do this in some form or fashion?" The mark of a great leader is not just self-awareness, but more of a "challenging self-awareness," someone who is always seeking more understanding of their own performance and how they can improve on a consistent basis.

Everyone can be a leader, but it seems only a few are committed to being the best leader through self-development on a consistent basis. Be one of those few and join me in eradicating weak leadership by being a bold, VELOCITY LEADER.

Kelly Castor

Chapter 1

Bold Leadership
The Need, The Reason, The Mission

bōld/

adjective

1. (of a person, action, or idea) showing an ability to take risks; confident and courageous.
2. showing or requiring a fearless daring spirit.
3. not afraid of danger or difficult situations
4. showing lack of fear
5. clear and distinct

The journey of becoming a Bold Leader begins now.

~ What is Bold Leadership and why do we really need it? ~

As the definition above outlines, bold leadership is all about courage. It's about having a fearless spirit. It's about meeting difficult situations directly with clarity. As you'll see throughout this book, it's about taking on some very specific traits and raising ourselves up to a higher level of leadership – a level that transcends techniques and tactics. It's a

1

framework that will expose the real leader within you. One that is confident and takes on challenges and opportunities with clarity and courage. In essence – it's about having the mindset and conviction to lead and do so with boldness. This is what Bold Leadership means.

The struggle is real. The rewards are immense.

~ The New President ~
He walked in, his face red and clearly not happy. "That was really uncomfortable for me." This was the new President of the organization speaking to the Sr. VP of HR. In the eyes of the HR Executive, the conversation being referred to was really inconsequential. It was just someone asking for clarity on a directive. The President hadn't been prepped, so he felt uncomfortable with being "put on the spot." Over the next several months she would start to get used to this type of interaction with this President. This was the beginning of a long process of operating with a Leader who lacked leadership strength. In fact, from a leadership perspective, he was weak. It was going to be a painful and long ride. The HR Executive knew it. She was a seasoned veteran with a strong track record of success. The pit in her stomach was something that she would get used to over the next 18 months. This was the beginning – the consequence of weak Leadership.

I could go on and on with real-life examples at every level of multiple organizations. As a Leadership Consultant, I've seen so many examples of weak leadership manifesting in a variety of ways that I could probably write a book that is nothing but one example after another. This is one of the main reasons I decided to write this book in the first place.

There's no shortage of leadership books on the shelves of any bookstore or at Amazon or any other book retailer, online or otherwise. This begs the question, "Why another leadership book?" To be candid, I struggled with this in terms of really deciding whether to write this book or not. I didn't want to write "just another leadership book." I wanted it to be different and impactful at a completely different level. Otherwise, what's the point?

What got me over the hump was how I continued to see good companies with good products or services, filled with good people, struggling with the most basic of things in terms of leadership. I also see this in my personal life. Societal issues. Organizational issues in services that I use daily. There is no lack of examples in so many facets of life that I've concluded that weak leadership adversely affects virtually every area of my life in one way or another. Don't let that line get past you, ***"Weak leadership adversely affects virtually every area of my life in one way or another."*** It affects your life as well.

Weak leadership has adverse effects on all of our lives on a daily basis. It's at the dry cleaners, restaurants, and coffee shops. When handling a question on your utility bill or lawn service. It's at the movie theater, grocery store, and possibly even your church. Should I even have to mention your job? It's at your company, your vendor's company, your client's company – it's virtually everywhere.

Because of my vocation, I know that I may be hyper-sensitive to it, but I firmly believe that what we have is nothing short of an epidemic in terms of weak leadership and how it imprints upon our lives. It causes more work for all of us. It causes stress we don't need. It consumes time that we are not spending on positive and productive things that are really important to us. It's a silent thief that invades our lives with extreme stealth and then manifests in palpable ways.

Think about your life. When was the last time you went to do anything and experienced a delay, a wrong order, a quality issue, or an experience that you know didn't feel was right, but you may not be able to put your finger on what was off about it? My belief is the overwhelming majority of those times were directly related to weak leadership at some point in the process. Leadership affects our entire lives, not just while we are at work, but while we are at other's work.

This put me on a mission to eradicate weak leadership. No kidding. I'm serious. I want to boldly proclaim that, *I'm on a mission to eradicate weak leadership by developing Bold Leadership. Leadership worthy of following.* This is why I decided to write this book.

Once I decided to write a book on leadership for such a bold reason, I realized that, once again, it upped the ante to not be just another book on leadership, but it needed to be worthy of such a lofty goal. This brought me to a rather interesting juncture. To accomplish that task, I needed to get everyone, or most everyone who reads this, to join me in the mission. To do this it requires, well… Leadership.

For anyone to follow you with any vigor, you must enroll them in a cause greater than themselves and certainly greater than their MBO's, KPI's or any other metric used to measure performance. You also must widen the net of potential followers because to do something big you need energy and mass. You can't do something big with small levels of energy. You need big, dedicated, and sustained energy.

The greater danger for most of us lies not in setting our aim too high and falling short; but in setting our aim too low, and achieving our mark.
- Michelangelo

So here I am at the beginning of this book and I'm asking something of you. I'm asking you to join me in this mission, this expedition, if you will. This brings me to a couple of core principles that we'll be going through in this book.

For anyone to follow and be thoroughly engaged in a cause, they must understand *Why* it is important to others and why it is important to them on a personal level. It must transcend the "work" level and touch us at our core for us to be truly engaged. This is, "The *WHY* is more important than the *WHAT*." As you'll see in the coming chapters, this phrase is utilized in a variety of ways and in different contexts. This *why* concept is not unique. In recent years, Simon Sinek [i] is probably most notable for focusing on the *Why*. I love Simon's work around this. It's impressive in how he lays it out for us to understand, but more importantly, it's impressive because of the affect it can have if we just adopt his teachings in tangible ways. This book will be an almost continuous lesson on the power of *Why*.

Another lesson is that leadership is not a zero-sum game. It would be great if you got everyone in your organization or on your team to be totally engaged. In fact, that should be your mindset, that you are working to enroll everyone at a very committed level. But you don't have to get everyone at that level to do extraordinary things. You just have to get most people at that level. The more you can get, the bigger, faster and more impressive the experience will be.

If you go back a couple of paragraphs, I said "To accomplish that task I needed to get everyone, *or most everyone*, who reads this to join me in the mission." As I said, the more the merrier, but I can tell you from personal experience that I have never gotten every person enrolled and engaged at the personal level I'm speaking of. But I have gotten enough that we were able to do some extraordinary things. I've also been a witness to this both from afar and with my clients. It's a beautiful thing, and it's never a zero-sum game.

Velocity Leadership is not just about being bold as a leader, it's about being bold about eradicating weak leadership. To do this, we need to understand key disciplines of leadership and also learn practical strategies and tactics, so we can not only be an effective leader, but also create more leaders in the process. So, let's join together and do something of positive magnitude. Let's do our part to eradicate weak leadership. Let's be a strong leader, eradicate weak leadership, and be bold in that endeavor – let's be Bold Leaders!

So, will you join me on this mission to eradicate weak leadership? The stakes are high. The work is real. The payoff is extraordinary. It's going to take Bold Leadership!

~ The Missing Ingredient ~

What you've been told as the most important aspect of leadership is probably not true. This isn't an intentional misleading. It's an understandable mistake. Understandable or not, it's undermining your ability to truly lead people with lasting impact.

When you are hired or promoted to lead a team of some sort, it is usually couched in some version of how excited the hiring party is for you to execute, to hit numbers, to grow market share, to exceed goals. It's all about output, results, performance – *achievements!*

The stage is now set: your job as the leader is to hit goals, increase market share, and take your group to the next level. What comes next is performance reviews, spreadsheets, actual-to-projected numbers, marks hit, and marks missed. If you are on or above target, accolades come your way. If you are below by a little, nudges of dissatisfaction. If you are way off your numbers, nudges turn into dissatisfaction and feelings of "get it corrected or we'll find someone who can."

This is an understandable situation and conversation. Businesses have to sustain themselves. They have a responsibility to owners, shareholders, employees, and their customers to be viable now and into the future. You can't be viable if you can't sustain yourself as a business. If you can't sustain yourself, well… you are out of business.

But what's missing in all of this are some basics. My first 5 or 6 years of leading people I never thought of asking myself, and nobody ever asked me, "Why do you want to lead?" In all my years of working with leaders, I've yet to have someone really have a solid, thought-out answer to that question. Most times I either get something like, "Because, it's my role." Or, "I'm the owner." Or, "That's what I was hired to do." Conversely, I also get the response of, "Hmm. I've never thought of that." I'm convinced that regardless which of these common responses I receive, the real answer for most of us is, "I've never thought of that." Why? Because most of us either aspire to or receive the opportunity to "lead" focused on achieving something. The achievement may just be the seat – the role and title of *boss*. This is by far the weakest reason to lead, but actually the most common. This is, again, a natural occurrence. It's about moving up and progressing our careers. There is nothing wrong with this thinking at all. It's what you want out of employees for the most part.

Chapter 1

"Carol, we are so excited that you've accepted the promotion to lead the sales team. With your track record of success, we are confident that you'll be able to rally the troops to hit the numbers we need!"

When we focus on results first, we have a much harder time attaining those results. This brings challenges. By focusing on the question, "Why do I want to lead?" we are starting to tap into the key missing ingredient of being an effective leader.

Leadership is about helping those within our charge. To help them rise up, to grow, and prosper within the endeavor. What we've learned is that to be an effective leader, a Bold Leader, you have to tap into a purpose that is well beyond the results. Answering the question, "Why do I want to lead?" is helping you define a purpose that is worthy of someone following. This requires the leader to work on themselves first through disciplines and become clear on their purpose of being a leader. The 3 Disciplines of Velocity Leadership are Purpose, Impact, and Achievements. As you can now see, *Purpose* is the first Discipline of Velocity Leadership. *Achievements*, or results, is the last discipline of Velocity Leadership.

"Definiteness of purpose is the starting point
of all achievement."
- W. Clement Stone

From the start, for most of us managing or leading anyone, it was presented and monitored exclusively in the realm of results. Here's the goal, what did you achieve? But as we dive into the 3 Disciplines of Velocity Leadership, your results are actually the last focus. They are not less important than what we've been told, but last in terms of syntax to achieving them. We must master the disciplines of Purpose and Impact first. By doing this, your ability to achieve and sustain outstanding results is much greater.

Let's dive into the 3 Disciplines of Velocity Leadership, and you'll begin to understand the flow and power of its design.

~ 3 Disciplines of Leadership ~

Leadership begins with YOU, the Leader. Leadership ends with YOU, the Leader. Leading people is not about YOU, the Leader. Wait. What? You are probably thinking, "Leadership starts and stops with me but has nothing to do with me? How does that work?" Great question.

To be a great leader, one of the key understandings is being clear on the *Why*. As I referenced earlier, at Velocity Leadership we say, "The *Why* is more important than the *What*." In this context, it highlights 3 disciplines of *Why* as it relates to "being a leader." I'll briefly highlight all 3 and then focus on Discipline #1 in more detail.

The first discipline is *Purpose*. Why are we leading in the first place? How do we define true meaning in being a leader? How we determine and utilize this meaning has a great impact on the effectiveness we bring to any situation as the Leader. We must be clear on "why" we are leading. Defining a clear purpose for ourselves is what drives our ability to stay focused on the "appropriate versus the urgent" perspective. It's not an exercise to be taken lightly. It sets the tone for everything we do. It's what gives us strength during challenging times and keeps us on track during the inevitable distractions of life.

The second discipline is *Impact*. How are we positively impacting those we are leading? How are they benefitting and growing due to our leadership and involvement? Our ability to develop people in a way that is of true, positive meaning to them is the personal, one-to-one relationship. This relationship is what gives us the opportunity to earn their "following." This drives sustainability in our joint endeavors. This supports a key requirement of being a great leader – you have to develop other leaders. This leader development is what extends your reach when you are leading an organization that is too large for you to develop a deep, personal relationship with everyone.

The third discipline is *Achievement*. What are we accomplishing in relation to our goals, our tangible metrics? This tends to get the most attention. If you are brought in or promoted to a leadership position, what results can we expect from you? Although I believe this is in some ways the least important, it's also in many ways the most important in terms of being able to have a platform to continue to serve and grow as a leader.

The combination of these 3 Disciplines – Purpose, Impact and Achievement – manifests in Who you are "Being" as a Leader.

~ Leadership Disciplines in Action ~

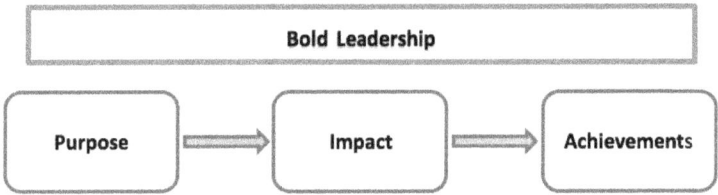

John Maxwell has defined Leadership as *influence* in his books and talks for many years. He dedicates the entire first chapter of his book, *Developing the Leader Within You 2.0*[ii] to this definition of Leadership. If you truly want to be an effective leader, you must develop a strong influence. If you focus on being clear on the meaning behind the 3 Disciplines of Leadership – Purpose, Impact, and Achievement – you'll have a greater influence for the right reasons.

"If you wouldn't follow yourself,
why should anyone else?"
-   John C. Maxwell

Who you are "being" as a Leader is what gives your words and actions power and *influence*. The combination of these 3 Disciplines defines who you are "being", and you must tap into these if you are serious about being a highly-effective leader, a Bold Leader.

I think it's important here to dive into the definition and perception of the word "discipline." Many times, whether it's used as a verb or a noun, discipline activates a negative feeling or emotion. As a leader, it's important to reframe this definition and to help others do so as well.

Discipline doesn't have to be associated with some sort of corporal punishment, even if it is a verb. Discipline is actually about success. If you want to get better at anything, you must be disciplined in your approach. If you want to be in better shape, you must be disciplined about what you eat and how often you exercise. If you want to be a better communicator, you must be disciplined in active listening and concise in sharing your thoughts. The path to success is lined with disciplined focus and effort.

"Discipline equals freedom."
-   Jocko Willink

Effective leaders view discipline as a necessary component to any worthwhile goal. It's an integral part of growing. If you want to improve an area of your life, you need to first acknowledge it. Second, come up with a strategy (actions) to improve and then implement your strategy consistently – a.k.a., with discipline. If you think of it that way, discipline is truly the key to success. It's not the only component, but it's a necessary one. You really can't achieve anything worthwhile without it. So let's embrace it as the positive it is rather than dread it as if we are some child who knows they are about to "get what's coming to them." Discipline is your friend. To quote Jocko Willink, "Discipline equals freedom!"

In terms of Velocity Leadership, the disciplines described are nouns. But to actually lead people, it will take discipline, the verb, to have any real impact. Bold, definitive actions based upon sound principles, carried out with relentless discipline, equal success. By doing this, we will be replacing weak leadership practices with Bold Leadership successes.

<u>Chapter 2</u>

Discipline 1 - *Purpose*
The "Deep Dive"

Purpose - this is truly the heart of the matter. It's about your calling. There is plenty of debate around finding your purpose, your reason for being on the planet. Since the recording of history, humans have always struggled with the nagging question, "Why are we here on earth? What am I here to do? What's the purpose of life? More importantly, what's *MY* purpose? Is it to just, *eat, sleep, work, procreate, get old, die? Is that it? No other reason?*"

In the 5th century B.C., Socrates' famous quote, "An unexamined life is not worth living" applies, especially if you are serious about being a leader. Taking the time to examine your *Why* for being a leader in the first place is paramount to your success and, ultimately, your happiness. For those reasons alone, it should encourage us to spend some time really thinking about why we are leading. Why are we worthy of someone's commitment to follow?

By definition, to be a Leader, you must have followers. To have followers, you must be worthy of following. That "worth" comes from you, your motivations, and internal reasoning for being a "leader." Your motivations will then manifest to the world in conjunction with your values. Combined, this is *who you are.*

15

"Managers work to see numbers grow.
Leaders work to see people grow."
-   Simon Sinek

This is probably a good time to talk about the difference between being a boss and being a leader. I know many bosses who aren't leaders. Conversely, I know many leaders who aren't bosses. Don't get confused in answering questions about your motives and reasons by thinking about hitting numbers and achieving objectives. We'll get to those areas soon, but I think you'll find that those results are directly related to understanding and acting *through* your clarity of purpose. When it comes to Discipline 1, Purpose, results are a by-product, not a motivator. Clarity around purpose is proportional to your level of success as a leader.

~ We all want to be part of something bigger than ourselves ... ~

To begin the process of defining our purpose as a leader, we must look at the human condition. We aren't leading computers, spreadsheets, or companies. We are leading people. This requires us to think about the basic needs and desires of humans. *I believe that all humans have an innate desire to be part of something bigger than themselves. They want to contribute to this cause. They want to know their contribution matters. And to some extent, they want to be recognized and rewarded for that contribution.*

Please don't skim past the above definition. It is foundational to tapping into a part of you, your purpose, that is essential to leadership excellence.

Let's dissect the previous statement so we can better understand it for the purposes of better serving our people and accomplishing our mission.

"We all want to be part of something bigger than ourselves."

What is it that drives us to make an effort, to care, to engage? At some level, true engagement almost always taps into this innate desire. This pull towards being part of something bigger. This desire has us searching very deep levels of our being, such as our belief in the life beyond or the lack thereof and our search to the ultimate question of "Why am I here? What is my specific purpose? What are my unique talents and how do I fit into the overall master plan?" In my opinion, all of these questions are valid and each of us needs to continue on this journey. Finding meaning in life is a much bigger topic than this book and would require someone with much greater insight than I possess. But if we take this quest and bring it down a couple of notches to our vocation and how we gain meaning and purpose in that area of our lives, it stands as a critical component when we take on the responsibility of leadership.

If we are going to assume that all humans want to be part of something bigger than themselves, it seems that our purpose should be connected to this. From a practical standpoint, it makes sense. We all have this *want* to be part of something bigger. So why not align our purpose with something that we know is present? It's a common denominator. Our purpose needs to be centered around helping people fill this need, this desire. Ultimately, as a Leader, we need to help people experience this connection with our goal or mission. We must tap into this innate desire and need. If we drill down a little deeper, the over-arching purpose is to *help* people.

Ah, this is the heart of the matter once again. Our purpose is to *help* people. Helping people tap into this *wanting* to be a part of something bigger than ourselves is a powerful, common thread.

They want to contribute to this cause.

When leading anyone or any group, a critical step is engagement. How do we get their attention in a way that *engages* them in thought and action? In essence, how do you get them to *want* to engage? This is the second important word in this sentence – want, *a want to contribute.*

Not only do they want to engage, they don't want to just passively engage, they want to *contribute*. So why would they want to contribute? Because the *cause* means enough to them that they "want" to. Another term for this is motivation. If they "want to" you don't have to "motivate" them to do it. The level of this self-driven motivation is directly related to the value they place on the cause. As a leader, it's our responsibility to *help* them see the link between what they value and the cause we are all working in and on. I'm going to address employee engagement later in more detail. But in terms of 'wanting to contribute', it's all about having them see the link between what they value and the cause we are dedicated to in their work.

They want to know their contribution matters.

This transfers the value *of* the cause to their value *to* the cause. In other words, self-value. This isn't their entire self-value, nor should it be. It's their self-value in relation to this cause. The more the cause resonates with them, the more value they will place upon the need to *know* their contribution matters. As a Leader, it's not only our responsibility to define the cause in a way that is meaningful, but to also make sure people understand how their contribution fits into the overall efficiency and effectiveness of the cause. Then they will *know their contribution matters.* Again, as a Leader, it's our responsibility to *help* them know, without a doubt, that their contribution matters.

And to some extent, they want to be recognized and rewarded for that contribution.

Recognized is the key word here. As a Leader, we must recognize people's contribution. How we do this is based upon who we are recognizing. Have you ever recognized someone in public for an outstanding job and watched that person whither and almost try to melt into themselves? Some people really don't like public recognition. It doesn't mean we won't ever recognize them in public for a job well done. It means we need to do it in a way that fits their personality. Some people love all the fanfare. Others prefer a handshake and a heartfelt smile. Others want the parade.

*"The deepest craving of human nature is the
need to be appreciated."*
- William James

Whichever way we do it, we must understand that recognition is part of the innate common denominator. Recognition and reward fuel the energy necessary for the long-haul and serves to re-engage people in remembering that they are a part of something bigger than themselves, and that cause means something to them. As a leader, we want to *help* them refuel and reenergize around the cause. Matching this with the innate desire to be recognized for their contribution is a natural and necessary component in helping people refuel. In this way, we can achieve the ever-elusive sustainability that all causes and businesses need to be truly successful.

We can't leave the area of *Purpose* without revisiting and highlighting the "want to help" area. I emphasized the word *help* in dissecting the statement on the innate human desire to be part of something bigger. You have to sincerely *want to help* others for the sole purpose of wanting them to grow and prosper and develop. This seems altruistic – and it is. But you utilize this altruism to focus on your *Why*, your purpose, your calling. If you think you are put on this planet to "hit numbers", then you are missing out on one of the most powerful and influential experiences in life – helping others be excellent at tapping into what they are put on the planet to do.

This takes us into the area of service. I love the term Servant Leadership. There have been many books and articles written on it. And with this has come debate about the impact and whether it's really the right way of looking at it. For me, it's common sense. When we are serving, we are coming as close to being selfless as we probably can. There is an internal reward that we get when we are serving. We've all probably experienced it. But we shouldn't look past it when we are talking about our purpose as a leader. Just as we are charged with fueling engagement of those that we lead, we also need to foster that within ourselves over and over. Perhaps we need more of this energy because we are the ones leading. A servant mindset helps us do this.

More than anyone I know; my wife epitomizes this. From everything to being a mother to feeding those less fortunate, my wife lives from a servant mindset. How can she help others with her gifts? How can she utilize her time, talents, and energy to help others? She operates from this perspective. Because of this, she's brought me into those experiences and I've had the pleasure of rediscovering the value of being selfless to whatever extent my ego allows. This isn't just a "feel good" thing. In fact, that's not it at all. It's more like getting closer to that ever-nagging question, "Why am I here?" It's hard to explain, but serving others brings out a part of our spirit that you just can't get any other way. Helping a homeless person with blankets on a cold night is much different than helping a team be engaged to accomplish a business task. But the essence of service and the power of a servant mindset is much the same. One may have more "humanitarian value" than the other, but my spirit recognizes it as being in the same neighborhood.

I believe that the premise of us all wanting to be part of something bigger than ourselves, wanting to contribute to the cause, wanting to know our contribution matters – it is truly a human thing, not a personality thing. Go help someone who is in real need and you'll understand that reward is not only important, it's present in an authentic and meaningful way.

To truly *help others,* you must give. Give of yourself. Give your time, your energy, your engagement to *help others* and you will receive it back ten-fold, provided you are doing it for the right reasons: to help others receive all they can from what they are doing in a meaningful and human way. This has to be at the heart of our Discipline 1 – Purpose.

Spend time working on your purpose as a leader. Ask yourself, "Why am I a leader?" Live with that question for a while. Spend some time jotting down answers to that question. Search, hunt, and find an answer to that question that motivates you beyond results or the physical rewards you may receive. Go deep. This is a critical step in being a leader of significance – A Bold Leader.

Chapter 3

Discipline 1 - *Purpose*
Bold Leader Character Traits

~ Self-Awareness ~

One common trait that virtually all good leaders depend upon is self-awareness.

Unfortunately, the absence of self-awareness is also a significant trait in weak leadership. I recently heard an executive speaking about himself and another peer by saying, "The one thing that we have in common is we are both 'UBER SELF AWARE'." This is usually a time when I cringe. Internally I want to run away from the conversation. It's almost like having someone emphatically tell you how humble they are. It's a big warning sign.

> *...first take the log out of your own eye, and then you will see clearly to take the speck out of your brother's eye. Matthew 7:5*

Inferred in the definition of self-awareness is the recognition that we have blind spots, flaws, idiosyncrasy's, as well as ineffective and unconscious habits – we all have them. A weak leader doesn't grasp this, let alone acknowledge it. A weak leader may not even believe that it's possible for them to have flaws, let alone have the willingness to look at and work on them. They just continue in their weakness.

An effective leader, a Bold Leader, not only understands this, but utilizes it to be on a never-ending quest for learning, for improving. They know they have areas of improvement and they want to be clear what they are and what they need to do to improve. They are always working on themselves first. Asking others their opinion. Asking, "How am I doing?" Sometimes it's audible and inquisitive. Other times it's internal, seeking their own assessment. But all great leaders are seeking better wisdom in developing their skills. They work hard on self-awareness.

~ Confidence ~

Self-Awareness, asking "How am I doing?" is not to be equated to second-guessing or unsureness. Great leaders, bold leaders, are confident. In fact, this never-ending inquisition into their own performance is where their confidence is rooted. It springs from the root of knowing they will always be getting better. Learning constantly.

One of the biggest fallacies of weak leaders is that they can never show vulnerability. That they want people to always believe that they have the answers, they are in control. But, in fact, their need to always "know" is what creates doubts in those they lead. The more they try to be the confident, "I have it figured out" type of leader, the more inauthentic and incapable they become.

Chapter 3

Bold Leaders are confident because they have done their homework. They've also fostered strong leadership relationships with those they lead. They've established a human relationship, one that shows we are all learning, we are in this together, and we are interdependent. This type of confidence mitigates any foray into the land of arrogance. It's still possible to slide into this land, but it is caught, isolated, and eliminated through the practice of self-development. It is displayed through the reality that they don't always know. They don't always have the answer.

But the confidence comes from knowing that they can arrive at the answer, the solution, by stepping into the breach with those around them and *leading* them to the answer or solution. This shows their "humanness" in a way that is inspiring to those they lead. It's authenticity on display in a very strong and confident way. By doing this, the leader becomes more authentically confident. By "being" more authentically confident, we inspire those around us to follow our leadership and also develop themselves at the same time.

If you pause for a moment and really think about this, you can see how by being a little vulnerable you actually foster confidence, and just as importantly, you display confidence. This results in developing more confidence in those you lead. Let that soak in.

Chapter 3

~ Integrity ~

Velocity Leadership is built around some core principles. One of the key models is what I call "The Three Powerful Truths." They illustrate one form of Integrity. I call this visible integrity. It's extremely important when leading others because it is visible to them. I outlined the 3 Powerful Truths in a book I co-authored with Mike Rodriguez last year called *A Better Plan,* published by Tribute Publishing. In short, The Three Powerful Truths are: Do what you say, when you say; Be who you want others to be; and Take 100% Ownership: good, bad or indifferent. These are critical behaviors to exemplify integrity.

As a leader, everyone is watching you. I'm always a little humored when I have managers or leaders come up to me and say things like, "I really watch my people" or "I keep a close eye on my employees." I typically smile and say something to the effect of, "Believe me, you aren't watching them nearly as much as they are watching you."

As a leader, we are always being watched. People are looking for confirmation of their beliefs. This is why visible integrity is so important. They have to believe and see that you will do the right thing, not the convenient thing or the self-serving thing.

Bold Leaders know that visible integrity is only as good as the strength of their private integrity. This "private integrity" is the key ingredient to authenticity and is perhaps the most important type of integrity. It's doing the right thing when no one is around to witness. You just do it because you believe it's the right thing to do. Without this, "visible integrity" is just a game. It's inauthentic and it will backfire. Everyone will see through it and you'll lose those you are trying to lead.

> *"Wisdom is knowing the right path to take.*
> *Integrity is taking it."*
> *- Anonymous*

This is why The Three Powerful Truths are only effective if you really mean it – if you are being authentic. You are displaying what is real through this method. It's not a tactic. It's a way of being. In building trust, there is no substitute for people knowing that you will consistently do the right thing regardless of the circumstance. Bold leader's step into the breach, are principled in their actions, and true to their team and themselves. They act as if no one is watching and it has no effect on their decisions. They are in integrity with themselves. By doing this, they are always visibly acting with that same integrity.

~ Gratefulness ~

It's one thing to be grateful in a reflective way. It's another to be grateful in a motivated way. Reminiscing is oftentimes an enjoyable event. There's nothing like talking with old friends about some of the experiences you shared together, or thinking of your family, young children now making their way as adults in the real world. Remembering what it was like when you and your spouse first dated – these are all good things, and in many ways, these memories massage the spirit in an enjoyable way. It brings a smile to my face just writing about it.

But gratefulness in terms of Bold Leadership is not a reflective exercise strolling down memory lane. It's an energizing experience that spurs us on to demand excellence of ourselves. To be grateful for the circumstances we are in and the people we are in them with. It drives us to walk a little faster and stand a little taller. We want to lean in to the opportunities. We want to go that little bit extra with those we are speaking with. It takes away the faint notions of "cutting corners" or thinking, "this is good enough."

"Thankfulness is the beginning of gratitude.
Gratitude is the completion of thankfulness.
Thankfulness may consist merely of words.
Gratitude is shown in acts."
- Henri Frederic Amiel[iii]

As a Bold Leader trait, gratitude is about increasing our energy. It's about taking intentionality to another level. It's about improving our own performance and that of those around us.

Before virtually every coaching session, presentation, or event that I do, I take a few moments to be thankful and grateful for the opportunity that I have right in front of me. I work hard at getting that gratefulness into my bones. I want to feel it. I want to really experience it. When I am able to do this effectively, there's a different "feel" to my work. This transcends me and fills those I'm working with or presenting to. There is a palpable difference in both experience and outcomes. This one act of "active gratitude" can take your current actions and behaviors and super-charge them. You and your people will notice the difference.

~ *Decisiveness* ~

Bold Leaders take action! Action that spurs growth, commitment, and movement towards the goal of the mission. One of the most disruptive and caustic impacts towards the growth and velocity of organizations is the act of inaction. The non-action of not making a decision and going forward has a huge negative impact on both productivity and morale. It's like being in stormy seas and then losing power. You become adrift, people start feeling out of control and that their destiny lies in circumstance rather than in their own hands.

*"More is lost by indecision than wrong
decision. Indecision is the thief of opportunity.
It will steal you blind."*
-   Marcus Tullius Cicero

Bold Leaders understand that they must offer direction and make tough decisions. They aren't afraid of failure for they will use that failure to go forward with more knowledge and intensity. They also know to involve their people in decision-making. They are confident in saying, "Let's figure this out. Who do we need to have in the room to give us the best possibility for a good decision?"

Once the facts have been gathered and those necessary have been conferred with, if there is no clear direction, they make the call. They decide. They own it. Because of this, the people around them will own it as well. They will own it in the way of "Let's make this happen."

As a leader, a Bold Leader, you have to have the confidence to make hard decisions. Much of this confidence comes in making an informed decision. But not all decisions are going to be clear cut. The rest of the confidence has to come in the form of "If it's the wrong decision, we will learn and adapt and come out better for it." It's a together type of thing. That's why it's so important to involve others and to have them see you "own" it.

The consequence of not owning it manifests in a way that has the leader becoming more interested in preserving their own reputation rather than promoting the feeling of, "we are all in this together." If this takes root in the organization, everyone is out to protect themselves because they don't feel like they'll be protected by the leader. When they see you, the leader, OWN it, they'll get behind you and feel responsible for the success of the decision.

Self-awareness, Confidence, Integrity, Gratefulness, and Decisiveness are all internally driven. They are the culmination of refining ourselves first and of striving for excellence within our own actions, behaviors, and practices. These are foundational building blocks of character. It's not everything involved in building character, but it's foundational. Without these traits, there is no way a leader can be strong. Weak leaders put on "airs" of having them. Bold leaders take on the work and dedication of developing them, turning them into who they are. If we are to eradicate weak leadership, we have to begin here.

It's not enough just to have these traits, this Bold Leadership Character. You have to funnel them into the next discipline. You must now take this from being "all about you" to being "all about them," those you are leading.

As we consistently work on ourselves, we must never lose sight of the fact that it's all for the purpose of serving others, helping them work on themselves. We must be the shining example, a light for them, to illuminate their path on the journey of serving others. This is why Bold Leaders understand that it starts and stops with themselves; it's all about the leader. But… it's not about you, the leader. It's about those you lead.

When you look back on your career, your points of pride, your legacy, if you will, it will not be defined by how much you grew personally. It will be defined by those you impacted and those who were impacted by them. But to have this be a legacy to be proud of, you have to become clear on your purpose. Work on developing the skills and behaviors necessary to fulfill that purpose and then channel that into everyone you lead with relentless pursuit.

You must be Bold!

<u>Chapter 4</u>

Discipline 2 - *Impact*
It's About Them

~ The call from Jimmy ~

I saw the call come in on my phone. I was on the other line working with a client. It was Jimmy O'Hare. I always smiled when I saw his name pop up on a phone call or email or whatever. I genuinely like Jimmy. I was authentically disappointed that I couldn't pick up the call. I finished up the coaching call about 30 minutes later and frankly had forgotten that Jimmy called. A little later I noticed a message waiting on my phone and got that same good feeling as I remembered, "Oh yeah, Jimmy called."

The voice-mail went like this, "Hey, it's your old friend Jimmy O'Hare calling. I owed you a call today. You are probably wondering, 'Why is O'Hare calling me today?" I guess we'll just jump to and call you old! The reason for that is, twenty-five years ago today I walked into a training class that changed my life and I just wanted to say thank you, sir. It was a great week and set the course for many great things.

*So, you **are** old and... THANK YOU! I hope you
have a great day!"*

Wow. I sat there with a smile the size of Texas on
my face and heart filled with humble gratitude. I was truly
surprised and humbled. It was one of the greatest feelings. I
know I keep using the word humbled. I don't want to
overuse it, but I can't think of any other way to capture the
feeling. The thought that I had any part in something that
was so significant in someone's life that they'd call me
twenty-five years later, to the day, to tell me we were in a
training class that I was leading and tie it to something as
profound as *"changed my life"* is, well... humbling.

I'm very happy to say this wasn't the first time that
I'd had someone from the past call me and thank me. In fact,
it wasn't the first time that Jimmy had called me to thank me.
But I want to be clear here. It never gets old. It never stops
humbling me. And probably most importantly, I never stop
being clear that it's not about me. I was a mere conduit for
those events. Those events are due to the folks calling. Not
me. If it was all about me then everyone I ever trained,
coached, or led would be calling me. But that doesn't
happen. It's only those who took something that came
through me and applied it to their lives in a way that made it
a life-altering event. This is all about them. Let me use some
more adjectives to describe these types of events.

Humbled, Proud, Moved, Joyful, Not worthy, Small,
Grateful.

Chapter 4

~ The Real Payoff ~

The payoff for effective leadership isn't money, notoriety, plaques, articles, books, trophies. It's the experience of being a small part of someone else's success, of being part of something that really matters beyond material things. In fact, it goes back to the key tenet for helping lead people to greatness. It's about being a part of something bigger than ourselves.

Go out. Take your knowledge. Turn it into action. Create an environment of engaging people in something bigger than themselves that is meaningful and worthwhile. Go be part of something bigger than yourself. Go be it for your sake and for those around you. There is no greater payoff than being a part of a tipping point that sets the stage for someone else to grow, to "Be A Leader" in their career, and more importantly, in their life!

This is what Velocity Leadership is all about – helping you develop into an even better leader, so you can help develop others. Perhaps they'll become great leaders that develop others. Or maybe they'll become great providers for their family and community. Or perhaps they'll be a great role model for others and turn their talents into even greater influence.

Leadership is something that you can continuously get better at. If you want to be a leader among your peers or lead a team or perhaps even an organization, the key to success is very simple: view Leadership development as a continuous effort on your part first (Discipline #1 –

Purpose) then work on your people. It doesn't work any other way. If you catch yourself focused solely on other's issues, on what they need to work on, fix, or develop, stop yourself and take a moment to ask, what are you doing to help them? What do you need to work on so you can support them in their improvement? It's so easy to get focused on what needs to be fixed that we start to lose sight of what we need to work on internally. To work on ourselves first allows us to support them in their growth, to work on their areas of improvement.

Although we have to start with ourselves, we always must remember and be motivated by the fact that it's not about us. It's about those that follow us and others around us. Calls, like I received from Jimmy, are not why we are leaders, but great reminders to be grateful for the opportunities to serve others in a way that results in a positive, lasting impact. By doing this, we have hopefully started a domino effect that spreads out exponentially.

> "The way to develop the best that is in a person
> is by appreciation and encouragement."
> -   Charles Schwab

When you think about it, one of the greatest legacies you can have as a leader is that you played a significant role in developing other leaders. This is what Discipline #2 is all about really. It's having *impact* on other people's lives. We'll delve deeper in how to do this in a later chapter, but it's important to remember that as a leader we are measured, in large part, by the effectiveness of those around us. It only makes sense that we work hard at having a positive impact on others so they can grow in ways that support their families, their careers, and those they are in contact with every day. To do this, we have to be *bold* in our intentions and *human* in our approach.

Having a positive, lasting – potentially life-changing – impact on others must be at the heart of our leadership focus. It's all about them. It's true we have to first get clear on our own purpose for leading, but in our actions, it needs to be about the development of our people. If you focus on having this type of meaningful impact on your people, then Discipline #3 – Achievement, will come with much more ease and significance.

> *"Non nobis solum nati sumus. (Not for ourselves alone are we born.)"*
> — *Marcus Tullius Cicero*[iv]

~ Being a Mentor ~

As a Bold Leader, we are always mindful of helping those around us grow. Stretching them. Challenging them. We live with the question, "How do we help them go from here to there on their growth path?" We need to pull out things in them that they may not even see in themselves. I've been fortunate over the years to have bosses and mentors who saw things in me that I didn't even see. And more importantly, they challenged me to uncover them, hone them, and work on them. They wouldn't let me get away with "getting by." At times that was painful. I was not always a willing student. I was, at times, defiant. But I was blessed with Bold Leaders. Leaders that wouldn't back down on demanding the pursuit of excellence.

Early in my career, I worked for a man named Dan. I was 22. Dan was in his early 60's. He'd been a salesman for so long that he still called himself a "peddler." This was a common and respectful term for a professional salesperson in his day. He worked mainly in the manufacturing world selling parts and supplies to a variety of industries. In some ways, it was blue-collar selling. Lots of handshakes, great stories, slaps on the back and an occasional bottle of spirits as Christmas gifts to his clients. Dan was a strapping guy even when I worked for him. I was a fit 22-year-old that had worked construction for several years. I was no stranger to a hard day's physical work. I was young, strong, and strong-minded. From a physical standpoint, I feared Dan and was certain that even in his 60's he could take me to task. He was not subtle nor smooth. He was direct, and, let me tell you, certain he was right... always. The fact is, he was right the overwhelming majority of the time.

Dan hired me to be the outside sales rep for a 5-store Auto Parts operation. He introduced me to the owners of the chain and said, "This is the guy that's going to make the difference in our growth." I was shocked – then scared. I had some previous sales experience, but had no idea what I was about to get into. I thought I did. But I didn't. The key here is that Dan saw something in me that I didn't. Once he proclaimed it to the owners, he was determined that I tap into it and use it. We had more than one go-around about my sales performance and sales habits. He taught me more and got more out of me than I even knew I had. As tough as it was, as unrealistic as I thought some of his expectations were – Dan was one of only a handful of people that I can point to who had a life-altering impact on me. If he were alive today, I'd be calling him just like Jimmy called me.

Who in your life has had this type of influence on you? Think about it. Come up with those people who had a life-altering impact on you and your career. Once you've done that, ask yourself this: Who is right in front of you that you have the opportunity to be that positive force for? Who do you have the opportunity to tap into their undiscovered talent and demand excellence from in a manner that when they look back on their life, you stand as one of those that had great influence? This is another important question that Bold Leaders live with. They check the answer often so they can be clear on how to have a real impact on those they lead and those around them.

~ *What do you want from me?* ~

He sat there, not happy, wondering, "Why? Why do I have to do that?" He was an excellent sales rep. He was hard-working, a team player, and wanted to excel not only in the company, but in his career. He was serious about it. I loved having him on the team. I also had times where he was a royal pain in the keister! But he was well worth it. If I had it to do over again, I would've invested more of myself in him.

To answer his question of, "Why do I have to do that?", I told him that people in the office watched him. In some ways, they looked up to him. In other ways, they watched him to see what he was doing.

He wasn't really buying it. He got it, but didn't want to get it, because he was focused on himself at that moment. This wasn't a common thing with him. He thought of others often. Don't get me wrong. He was competitive. He wanted to win, to sell more than everyone else. He liked how that felt. He was jovial, but he also liked having "bragging rights."

So I brought him into some reality. "Dale, I need you to do this because others are watching you. Even though you are hitting your numbers, it's more important for you to follow the procedures more than anyone else in the company." He didn't particularly like that explanation. I added, "You are a leader." He quickly retorted, "I don't want to be a leader!" To which I replied, "You don't have a choice. That was decided long before you started shaping your own life. You were a leader from the day you were born. Now the question is, do you want to live up to that potential or not?" Dead silence.

After what seemed like five minutes (which was probably more like 30 seconds,) his frown melted into his big smile and he said, "Being a leader was decided long before I started thinking about it. I like that."

Chapter 4

~ The Key to Demanding Excellence ~

The moral of the previous story isn't that you need to follow procedures. It's much deeper than that. The real story begins back at the beginning, with "What do you want from me?"

Oftentimes I witness Owners, Executives, and Leaders wanting people to follow them with exuberance, commitment, and the intangible of "going the extra mile" because they want to… they really want to. But they've never taken the time to really engage them in the mission, the cause, the '*Why*'. Oh, they are sure they have taken the time and effort. *They have a great on-boarding program. They have a great training program. They have clear-cut goals and roles.* I've heard it all. And even though they may have those things, typically they aren't always great. Additionally, that's not really what I'm talking about. I'm talking about what shapes all of those things. What gives those things deeper meaning and influence on everyone.

Think of it this way:

If I was speaking at your company event and I walked on stage after a brief introduction and I started by asking everyone in the room to follow me. "I'm on a mission. I want you to follow me. Who's in?" How many people do you believe would raise their hand? How many people out of those that did raise their hand would be willing to follow me no matter what? How many would give me their all, work harder and longer than they ever had before, be more committed than ever before, be in it for the right reasons, throw themselves into it with all the energy and commitment that they could muster, and keep going until we achieved our goals? Answer: probably nobody. Why? Because they don't know where we are going and, more importantly, *why* they should be a part of it.

This is one of the most underrated and overlooked steps in developing a high-performance organization, one that is about growth and sustainability. We have to get clear on the "why" behind the "what" and communicate this consistently to our people. Then we translate why it's important to them, not just why it's important to the company. If we do this effectively, we begin the process of engaging them into "being" versus doing.

This is leadership in action. It's not theoretical. It's not musing. It's not "knowing." It's a way of "being." Just like we must engage them into "being versus doing," we have to engage ourselves into "being" a leader worthy of following. This is the only way we can ever have the type of positive impact on them as a professional, and more importantly, as a human that we are striving to be. This striving to be of a significant, positive impact for our people is an integral practice, or habit, of being a Bold Leader.

Another important point from the "what do you want from me" vignette is that I was demanding excellence in terms of what he was asking of himself. He had it in him, but he was coasting. He was looking for a shortcut, a way out. But excellence demands higher internal standards than external. In other words, his level of acceptable performance had to be higher from an internal perspective than anything that I could impose on him.

How many times have you thought or heard someone say, "No one is harder on me than me." This is the internal perspective I'm talking about. But as a Bold Leader, we can't allow someone to slide on this. At times they need us to remind them of the standards they need to hold themselves to, not because of results, but because of who they are and what they have to offer. We must demand that they look in the mirror and live up to their own standards. If their standards are too low, then we need to help them have higher standards.

I've found that the overwhelming majority of people have higher standards in them. Sometimes they just need some reminders and support to tap into them – to demand it of them. This is what we do as leaders. We help people find or rekindle potential and the need to maximize it. If we are going to lead people to the extraordinary, we have to expose and demand excellence of ourselves and our people.

Our ability and desire to have a positive, lasting impact for those around us is a critical discipline. Bold Leaders embrace the responsibility of having lasting *Impact* on those we lead.

Chapter 5

Chapter 5

Discipline 2 - *Impact*
Bold Leader Traits, Motivation, & Habits

~ The Interview and Beyond ~

I remember her in the interview, timid, small, a little shy. But there was an underlying confidence that I don't think she even saw in herself. It was a puzzling event for me as I had interviewed hundreds of potential salespeople at that point in my career and was very clear what I was looking for and reasonably adept at being able to recognize it. On the surface, she wasn't really exhibiting the traits that fit our profile. But there was something about her that intrigued me.

A year or so later I was sitting there listening to her, noticing her stature, her confidence. She still seemed a little soft-spoken, but there was a confidence that filled not only her, but the entire room. In some ways, I couldn't have been prouder. In another way, I remember being astounded and impressed. A year or so after that, she was leading a sales meeting for her team, in her office. She was not just a sales manager. She was a sales leader. Awesome.

What really happened here was not just a story of me being aware and noticing the difference. It was much more than that. It was perseverance on her part. She struggled at times. I remember having conversations with her where she wasn't sure she was going to make it. I, at times, shared that thought: she might not make it. But I could always see this underlying confidence in her that needed to be released. I'm not really sure how it happened. We kept working. I should say, SHE kept working. She went from timid to competent to confident to leader.

It was humbling to be even a small part of that story. To this day, she is a leader of considerable force. I can only imagine how many people she has positively impacted since those days. No doubt, it's been many.

~ *Develop First, Train Second* ~

But what is the difference between those who move into leadership positions and survive compared to those who lead teams or companies to extraordinary successes? It's not just a singular thing, but one trait I've found to be present in most is the adoption of the mindset, *Think Development First, Training Second.* This is not to imply that you don't need to train. You absolutely need to train. The distinction lies in what you attach to training versus developing. Training is teaching someone how to "do." Developing is teaching someone how to "be." When we take on the "Develop" mindset when it comes to having impact with our people, we start with them first, then we go to what we need them to do.

Chapter 5

Think of it this way. If you are going to teach someone how to conduct an interview from a training perspective, we give them the tools by giving them an interview guide with questions to ask, ways to look at a resume, and perhaps even ask them to determine if they think the candidate will fit in with the culture or compare their previous experience with the position they are interviewing for. All good training. Now think of how you might do this thinking of developing first. Perhaps you would start with what the interviewer is projecting. Who do they need to "be" to portray our culture properly? Teach your employees how to greet others, how to shake hands, and how to carry themselves - deportment. Then you might get into some of the questions they need to ask. Instead of just having them read questions, start asking them to tell you why they think we are asking this question, then the next. Help them understand what the company is looking for in those questions. Then you give them permission to dig deeper if they don't feel like they've gotten what they need out of that question. This is developing first, training second. This is done not necessarily in a sequential manner, but in a positional manner. We are operating from the position of developing versus training.

Thinking that your role is to develop versus train is a powerful trait to turn into a habit. It's an essential trait for Bold Leaders. If you recall, many of the traits we talked about in Discipline 1 – Purpose, were considered "internal." Meaning they were primarily drivers to our values and beliefs that created powerful habits. They were tools and convictions we used as an internal compass to keep us on the path of continuous development and growth.

Chapter 5

Developing the trait of 'Develop first, Train second' is internal in terms of consciousness but external in terms of actions. It becomes a discipline in terms of a verb – you have to act it, not just think it.

Another example of how this trait manifests is in terms of how you look at your team in general. Many times as leaders we are focused on production in one form or another. If you are in IT, it may be in terms of builds, tests, and launch dates. If you are in sales, it is likely in activity numbers, pipelines, and sales numbers. If you are leading a company, it might be a focus on market share, actual to forecast, EBITDA, etc.

Whatever the metric you are focused on, how you get your team to hit the mark is a driver to much of our thinking. This type of thinking is understandable and doesn't need to stop. But if you start to adopt the 'Develop, first, Train second' mindset, you start asking different questions of yourself and your team. Instead of asking what people need to do, we go about it a little differently. We get clear on the outcome we need, including what people need to do to accomplish the goal. Bold Leaders then force themselves to dive a little deeper and ask, "Who do they need to be to accomplish the task?" instead of "What do they need to do to accomplish the task?" Let's be clear, we aren't going to forget what they need to do, and most likely, neither are they. So, this isn't an "either/or." It's an "and," meaning we are going to focus on who they need to be to accomplish the goal, i.e., "do" the task and hit the timeline.

~ *Who We Are* ~

An example of how you can utilize this mindset is to adopt part of the Velocity Leadership system – the developing of an empowering *Who We Are* mindset. This is a way of describing *Who We Are* as a team, department, or organization. It's usually three to five bullet-points and it captures the essence of who we are "being" as a team. Sometimes it's descriptive of our current state. Other times it's aspirational. Many times, it has elements of both.

This is a powerful tool that helps us keep present who we need to be to not only accomplish our tasks, but what we rely upon to do it consistently with excellence. One way to look at it is that it's your group's true north – it's your compass to make sure your company isn't getting lost in the forest of "doing and output."

Oftentimes we use the *Who We Are* process to capture what attributes got us to the level of our current success, so we don't lose those qualities as we scale. Just like people, the *Who We Are* has to grow as we scale to new heights with new challenges. But the core of *Who We Are*, our principles, do not change. They are foundational, and we must protect them from the apathy of familiarity and the death grip of new status, power, and opportunity. In some ways, it's about remaining humble. But in other ways, it's about harnessing the power of our principles, so we can charge into the future to new heights and new levels of success.

At Velocity Leadership, we utilize the process of *Who We Are* as the foundation of a larger initiative. This ranges from a company-wide, High Productivity Culture Initiative, to a team or department Productivity Improvement Program. The process is the same, it's just implemented at a different scale. Even if we implement this as a company-wide initiative to gain the maximum value out of it, we still create mini *"Who We Are's"* so we can tap into specifics of a function or department in a way that feeds the larger, corporate mission and purpose.

The purpose of creating a *"Who We Are"* is to have a motivating standard that captures the essence of the *Why* of the company in a way that highlights behaviors versus tasks. It aligns beautifully with thinking 'development first, training second'.

Briefly, the steps to creating a compelling corporate *"Who We Are"* are as follows:

- Define the company *Why* in a way that represents the human meaning behind your work.
- Define the key behaviors and mindsets necessary to reach extraordinary levels of success.
- Roll out to the organization with a strong emphasis on *why the company exists and why it matters to the employee.*
- Proactively and consciously get the *Who We Are* into the work. (This is critical to sustainability.)
- Utilize the *Who We Are* to reward positive behaviors and correct non-productive behaviors.
- Live it… every day, every way.

Chapter 5

~ Defining the Company Why ~

Earlier I referenced Simon Sinek's work on this in recent years. I would highly suggest you view his TedTalk entitled, *"Start with Why – how great leaders inspire action."* It's a great illustration of the power of having a compelling *Why* for your organization. To define this is an exercise that ranges from group frustration to exhilarating discovery. This is typically done with the entire leadership team of an organization. It takes several sessions to uncover, distill, and encapsulate a compelling *Why* for the organization in a way that can be used to develop a tagline for the corporate *Who We Are*. The tagline says what we do, but it has limited power if people aren't clear on *Why* we do it and *Why* it's important to *them*. This step is not for the faint at heart and is an early test of conviction to the process for the leadership team. It's both art and science and takes a steady hand to come out of this first step in a momentous and united way.

Define behaviors, mindsets, and outcomes. This step moves from the *Why* into the *Who We Are*. To do this, we have to start thinking of behaviors and mindsets that help us fulfill our *Why* and how. The *Who We Are* is typically three to five bullet points that describe the types of behaviors and mindsets we want to achieve our goals. It's important to note that not every organization has a tagline. Many times, it's just as effective to have the *Who We Are* as the completed body of work.

Here are some examples:

Taglines: We level the playing field; We do the right thing, not the easy thing; We see solutions; We inspire healthier communities by connecting people to real food; We accelerate the world's transition to sustainable energy.

Who We Are: We Innovate, Advocate, We are Accountable; We are Better Solutions, Better Experience, Better Future; We are driven, Challenge the status quo, Go the extra mile.

Inspired Employees Are the Most Productive

PRODUCTIVE OUTPUT

SOURCE BAIN & COMPANY AND EIU RESEARCH, 2015   © HBR.ORG

At this point we can lose sight of the power of this because of the simplicity of the statements. In fact, when coupled with a strong process, the power and impact is due to the simplicity. We'll cover how to construct simple, yet powerful descriptors that motivate desired behaviors in a later chapter. The key takeaway here is that to tap into the collective *Who We Are* raises all boats, including the leader. What I mean is that it gives us a platform to raise the performance level of everyone – from the highest levels in the organization to the lowest levels. It's about bringing this mindset to all employees at every level in a way that has everyone (virtually everyone) raise their personal level of performance. This is a different way to view the term: Leaders at all Levels. This popular catch-phrase is not just for leadership skills meant to be employed with others. It's first and foremost for developing and implementing leadership habits within ourselves, regardless of position or role.

Obviously, just having a tagline and a bullet-point list of key behaviors is not going to magically improve performance. It's a framework for how we interact with others, how we monitor our own behaviors, and a way to keep this alive in our work on a daily basis with clarity. It takes a coordinated roll-out and significant development at the frontline levels of leadership. But the payoff is outstanding. A study[v] by Bain & Company[vi] concludes that "engaged" employees show a 44% increase in productivity over the "satisfied" level of employees. The study clearly identified the correlation of engaged employees, those that have a clear understanding of the *Why* of the company, and how it relates to the personal interests and values of the employee.

We'll delve deeper into this when we discuss Employee engagement, but to embrace this understanding as a tangible way to improve employee productivity in a consistent and sustainable way is extremely important. It's a key distinction of Velocity Leadership.

Chapter 5

~ The One Thing ~

When thinking of someone at your employment or volunteer group or your circle of friends, have you ever thought, "Man, that girl has so much to offer. If she could just get over this *"One Thing"* (fill in the blank here) she would be so much more effective," or "better to be around," or "life would be so much easier for her and those around her," or a myriad of other possibilities. The first key to this is to be able to recognize the "One Thing."

It's not so much in knowing how to improve or fix the "One Thing". It's the art of identifying the "One Thing". If you are going to have a real *impact* on the people you lead and those around you, it's imperative that you are able to cut through the noise and identify the main thing that is preventing them from having maximum impact themselves. This takes you from just an improvement mindset – a way to get them to perform better in achieving results – to having a radical step forward in virtually everything they do. This is the power of identifying the "One Thing."

Chapter 5

~ The football player ~

He came in, a little brash, a little disheveled, but beaming with confidence. He was rough around the edges but carried an energy that you wanted to be around. He was an athlete. He played division 1 college football. He wasn't a big guy, but he was hard-nosed and showed a willingness to mix it up. From a personal standpoint, I liked him.

As I got to know Sam and observe his behavior, there was something about him that just wasn't right. He worked hard. He said the right thing at the office. But something was just off. At first, I was distracted by his appearance and wondered if that might be his "One Thing." His suits were always wrinkled and his ties were wrinkled with stains on them. His shoes were always scuffed up. He clearly needed someone to help him with some attention to detail in this area, but it wasn't just that. That wasn't his "One Thing".

As his sales started turning into customers, his "One Thing" showed up quickly. His attention to detail was so lacking that virtually every new customer he brought in had an issue of some sort – something wasn't explained, or it was explained away in an ambiguous manner. This was his "One Thing."

So the sloppy appearance wasn't Sam's "One Thing." It was a manifestation of his "One Thing." His need to take more time, to learn more, to be more precise, to handle questions and concerns from potential clients more thoroughly all pointed to his One Thing. His attention to detail and communicating those details effectively was his One Thing. You might be saying, "That's two things." Technically correct. Functionally incorrect.

The "One Thing" is about impact. What is the One Thing that could have the most impact on someone's career and life? In Sam's case, there was a telltale sign, his sloppy appearance. This wasn't his high-impact One Thing, but it sure did give us a hint at what it might be. To have a life-altering effect on Sam, we needed to go deeper. His habit of appreciating the "speed of the close" over clear, detailed communication was his One Thing and it showed up in his performance.

If you want to have a strong impact on those you lead, you have to find their One Thing and work on it. We all have it to some degree. This doesn't need to be a never-ending search for "what's wrong with them." This is about identifying key behaviors or actions that are getting in the way of performing with excellence.

So what do you do with this "One Thing" once you've identified it?

~ Facts, Nurture, Lead ~

Difficult or confronting conversations are something none of us like to have. But to be a Bold Leader, you must embrace this type of tension. You have to become adept at handling them in a way that continues to have an impact on the journey towards excellence.

In today's culture, we tend to talk around issues rather than to issues. Perhaps this has something to do with political correctness or just a natural desire that most of us have to not hurt anyone's feelings. Irrespective of the reason, Bold Leadership is predicated on the need to be genuinely and compassionately authentic with those around us. Without this, we could just call it "timid" or "avoidance" leadership. So let's be bold and compassionate by handling difficult conversations with a method that requires clarity and leadership… leadership as a verb.

This is where Facts, Nurture, Lead comes into play. It's a simple method of clearly getting to the point, being supportive, and motivating with clear steps to improve or enhance performance.

Facts – When you bring someone in to talk, open with why you are meeting with them. Here's an example:

"John, I needed to meet with you to talk about the way you are communicating with people in meetings, specifically in design meetings. What I saw in the last meeting is not acceptable and isn't helping you or the team. It's not Who We Are."

Chapter 5

Boom! It's clear, concise, and creates an environment that gives you the best opportunity for getting to tangible steps towards improvement. Another important factor is that if we don't get to the point right away, they don't hear anything you say. Many times, weak leaders call people in and start off a difficult conversation by saying things that are filler – typical avoidance blubber.

"John, you've been here for a year now. Ya know, you bring a lot of experience here. You've helped out a lot... I mean, we all can get better, right? So, uh, I wanted to bring you in and talk about something ... I mean, everyone admires your knowledge around here ... but, uh ... well, I was hoping we could talk about the design meetings – you know, your experience can really help us, but, uh..." You get the point. But what's interesting is when we do this, all of the words that we are using to talk around the subject are not only not effective, they aren't even heard.

What do you think John is thinking when the weak leader is blubbering around how people like you, respect you, etc.? He's thinking, *"Oh crap. Am I in trouble? Design meeting – what happened in the design meeting? What did I do? I didn't come up with those bad ideas. Am I getting fired? Who ratted me out? I bet it was Heather. She's been gunning for me since I got here."* It's a never-ending stream of rapid-fire thoughts, judgments and defenses.

Bold leaders understand that people have radar. They can feel that this isn't a normal meeting. They are already on edge, searching their memory for what this could be about. All of the preambles and "softening the blow" bluster doesn't work anyway and, in fact, causes the person we are talking with to lose focus on what we really need them focused upon. Therefore, open with the facts. Frame it out immediately.

Nurture – This is where you want to honestly tell people how their skills and talents are not equaling their impact. In other words, their behavior is mitigating their influence. When you mitigate your influence, you are not as valuable to the organization. If we've already tapped into the innate desire to be part of something bigger than themselves, we can remind them of this desire and that their contribution is not hitting the mark that *they* want to hit. Let's pick up the same example from above.

"… What I saw in the last meeting is not acceptable and isn't helping you or the team.

John, your experience and knowledge of our system is not being fully utilized because of your method of delivering, or communicating, that understanding to the people that need it. To describe what I saw in the meeting I would call it abrasive, brash, bordering on arrogant. Condescending is another word that comes to mind. My point is that you have lots to offer and it's getting lost in how you are offering it. We need to fix this. This is an area that you must improve if you are going to maximize your contribution here. Let's talk about some ways that I think you can work on your delivery, so you can be more effective."

At this point, there will certainly be more dialogue. It can go a lot of different directions. You might hear some excuses. You might have to give very clear details of what was said and how it came across. You might have to deal with some anger or defensiveness. But the key here is to stay clear on the facts and focus on their responsibility to contribute in a productive and meaningful way.

During the "nurture" section you also want to have some clear steps of improvement. In John's case, it might be that when he feels his emotions rising, he needs to use that as a trigger to "ask questions" rather than blurt out rebuttals or best practices in a condescending tone. He might need to work on respecting opinions that differ with his. A tool you can give him to work on that is to say, "Help me understand…" and then really listen to understand. There are a variety of things that may be useful. You want to come up with 2 or 3 key behaviors that he can start using right away. Then we move into the final phase.

Lead – This is where you need to turn the energy of a difficult conversation into a catalyst to move forward. You have to give them some confidence and energy to go be who you need them to be now. Let's continue on with our example of John.

Once you've outlined 2 or 3 things they need to do to be more effective, you wrap the conversation up something like this:

"John, I've seen you take your knowledge and experience and turn it into tangible impact to our process and deliverables. What we are talking about here is having your positive impact become the norm. This is about your contribution to our customers, company and our co-workers being that of an "A" player on a more consistent basis. This is something that you are not only able to do, but something that you and the rest of the organization deserves."

Chapter 5

Many people leave the conversation right there. And if you did that, you would be way ahead of the game of most leaders. But if you want to go the extra mile, if you want to be the true essence of a bold leader, you go one step further with a true differentiator. We call it, "This is how it will show up."

Let's continue with John.

" ...*This is something that you can not only do but that you and the rest of the organization deserves. John, here's how I'll know we are on the same page. (insert the behaviors you outlined earlier) When you are pressed in a meeting and think people are off-base, I'll hear you say, 'Help me understand ...' Or, you'll be asking lots more questions in a calm voice. This is how it will show up and I'll know we are on the same page and tracking forward. My goal here is to not have to have this conversation again except to only congratulate you on your progress. Fair enough?"*

This is a way to solidify the behaviors or actions you need to see for improvement in a way that is extremely tangible and will give you a clear path to either acknowledging the behavior change with John or remind him that he needs to employ the course correction outlined. It's either recognize the new behavior or correct his unchanged behavior. Remember to use, "This is how it will show up." It's a game changer for you and the person you are talking to.

To lead effectively after this type of conversation, we need to be looking for the behavior changes we asked for and acknowledge them when it happens. This reinforces the drive toward excellence and increases the *impact* of that person.

When having corrective, difficult conversations, we need to follow the model of Facts, Nurture, Lead. Then follow it up with "This is how it will show up." If we do this, we take a significant step forward towards having our people really *live* being a part of something bigger than themselves, contributing, know their contribution matters, and being recognized for that contribution. This is a strong foundational piece to having meaningful *Impact* with those we lead.

Chapter 6

Discipline 3 - *Achievement*
Your Seat at the Table

As I moved up the ladder and started managing regions versus territories, I became known as the guy that, "Wherever he goes, sales follow," meaning we grew and achieved revenue targets. At the time it was what I thought was most important. I didn't believe it trumped everything else. We still believed in taking care of our people. We achieved results with a high amount of discipline. We took care of each other. It wasn't to achieve the numbers at all costs. But it was very important. We didn't lose sight of them, and we were serious about achieving them.

Discipline 3 – Achievement, is exceeding expectations. It's all about hitting your numbers. It's what you were hired for. Grow this, build that, surpass milestones, exceed MBO's, etc. It's what people measure and what they look for. But this also sets the stage for improper syntax if you want to lead towards excellence. It's not that we shouldn't be focused on results. We absolutely should be. But Bold Leaders understand that the results are a by-product of their work, not the real work. It's a scorecard. It's an indicator of past efforts. By the time your metric is measured, your ability to change your performance is either impossible or virtually impossible. Meaning that your *influence* over performance is either significantly mitigated or rendered completely moot. In other words, it's too late. It's too late to do anything about the result.

Hitting your benchmarks feels good. It's something to be proud of. It's usually more public so it feels great, feeds the ego, raises our public stature, and opens opportunities for the future. It's where the public "you" lives. But if you attempt this without Disciplines 1 & 2, Purpose and Impact, there is no depth of foundation. If you don't have this foundation, your organization will implode.

Early in my consulting years, one key model that I used was highlighting the difference between "average" companies and "great" companies. One of the key examples of this was that in average companies the top salesperson basically ran the company. The numbers they produced were viewed as so important and necessary that they would circumvent policies, defy procedures and shortcut many of the steps in the process. This is what I mean by saying that the top salesperson basically ran the company. The only principle they had to stick to was the principle of producing sales. This causes so many issues in the organization that it's an entire book in and of itself. But when I speak of an implosion, it not only can come to the salesperson, but oftentimes to the organization as well.

Typically, this type of a situation arises in younger organizations that are still trying to gain a beachhead in their industry. But as the company grows and starts to establish itself, what becomes apparent is that there is no way to scale without having sound procedures and a cohesive philosophy to operate within. Without this, one-off deals, special pricing, and/or terms and a variety of other "unique" necessities to close a sale become unsustainable. This has one of two things happen most of the time. 1) The organization clamps down, weathers the storm of change, and begins to hire and train a new breed of top salespeople to perform their duties. 2) The salesperson who is not willing to adapt goes away. This is usually not a pleasant event. It plays out over months or even years. It causes mass disruption internally which steals energy from performance goals. It's costly, painful and... inevitable.

This is why we must focus on Purpose first, Impact second, and Achievements last. But achievement, in many ways, is a by-product of being really clear about Purpose & Impact anyway. To attain consistent and sustainable results – Achievements – we must be clear and present with *Why* we want to lead and be intentional in helping our people grow with impact.

In the world of selling, there's an old saying, "You can't manage results, you can only manage activity." This applies to leading anyone doing anything. In reality, you can only manage "to" something (Achievements) by focusing on vision and personal motivations (Purpose) combined with habits and development (Impact). The key here is syntax – it's the order of your focus. This is why we start with Purpose, flow into Impact, then, using habits and tactics, we attain results, Achievements. Before we start defining specific tools and activities that boost productivity, it's important that we talk about the environment that you create for your team or organization. This eco-system is a critical component to achieving the results you desire over the long haul. Although we believe that, in some ways, achievements are last in the line of focus, we also know that hitting your metrics are what gives you the opportunity to continue to lead. Setting the environment in a thoughtful and consistent manner is exactly what gives you the ability to not only hit your numbers, but it allows you to maximize the Purpose and Impact Disciplines to exceed your numbers in a sustainable manner. Think about that. It gives you and your organization the ability to *achieve or exceed your numbers in a sustainable manner.*

As a leader, that's the game you want to be in. As a BOLD Leader, that's the game you *demand* to be in. You demand it of yourself first, grow your people into demanding it of themselves, and then you achieve - over and over and over.

~ Velocity Leadership ~

So how does this eco-system really work? The name of my consultancy that I established in January of 2002 is *Velocity Leadership.* This is not because I just thought it was cool. It has a literal meaning and it describes what you want to create in terms of environment if you really want to out-perform your competition and achieve your goals consistently.

The rudimentary definition of velocity is Direction *plus* Speed *plus* Inertia. Inertia being defined as 'the absence of drag.' So if you break that down in a manageable way for business, it's Direction, *plus* Speed, *minus* Drag.

Direction – Clarity around where we are going and why.
Speed – Focusing on the right things and verifying this often.
Drag – Eliminating energy spent on things that are not driving us towards our goals.

~ Direction ~

In terms of environment and culture, clarity is essential. Not just clarity as to where we are going, but clarity on why we are going there and how we are getting there. Clarity, in many ways, from the perspective of leadership is a verb.

For years I've been a part of, or have witnessed, really good teams flounder in terms of progress due to lack of clarity. When you are part of an executive team, many times you spend countless hours working on strategy and execution with your peers. You can produce great work in terms of where you are going. You can spend time developing key internal execution strategies. You can spend hours identifying areas of the process that will need altering and discussing personnel around those. And then… you don't effectively communicate that to the organization with enough clarity to create the laser focus you need to compete at your best.

When focusing on *clarity*, we must spend what feels like an inordinate amount of time communicating our direction multiple times at multiple levels of the organization. It needs to take on "mantra-like" status. As you'll see in the coming chapters, to achieve and maintain a highly productive organization, you have to get clarity "into the work." This clarity goes beyond just knowing where you are going, but it starts there. Your direction has to be clear. If we don't have clarity, we are lost. To illustrate this, I use a technique that I call the *Mall Map*. Before apps, if you went to a mall that you weren't familiar with and needed to get something fast, you would find a physical Mall Map. To get in and out efficiently, you would find the mall map and look for the type of store or specific store that you wanted to go to. Once you found it, the next thing you had to do was to find the red dot or the green star that signified "You are here." Once you had both, you could map out the most efficient way to get there. But you have to have both of those points – where you want to go and where you currently are. It's the same thing with leading anyone anywhere. You have to clarify both of these for you to clearly define the direction you are going.

As a side note, knowing where you are right now may be one of the hardest aspects. Remember this: ***open, honest understanding and acknowledgment of where you truly are, not where you think you are, is the first step in achieving any worthwhile endeavor.*** You have to be clear about where you are and in terms of being a leader, where your people are. If not, you will spend your time reverse engineering processes, playing catch-up, and enduring unnecessary stress due to not having a powerful and objective understanding as to where you and your team are in terms of their output capabilities.

Clarity is a key ingredient to the first element of velocity: Direction.

Chapter 6

~ Speed ~

Adding the second element of velocity, Speed, is dependent upon processes. You can't out-produce the processes capacity. It's virtually impossible. If, by some miracle, you are able to out-produce the maximum capacity of your processes at some point, you can't sustain it for very long or it will break. Period. End of story. Think of the processes of an engine in a racecar. It is highly tuned, built for high output, sustained for a specific amount of time, say, 500 miles. Every now and then the driver can push it beyond its limits and not damage the engine so much that it can't complete the job at a high level of output. However, if the driver over-rev's the engine too many times for too long, he starts to lose overall output performance because of the stresses to the entire process and all the moving parts. If he keeps pushing its output, eventually something breaks. It implodes or possibly explodes, thus stopping all performance.

When it comes to people and processes, it is a continuous pursuit of excellence through improvement. We are always looking for ways we can do more and maintain high standards of efficiency. But we have to make sure we aren't over-revving our people or our processes. If we don't pay attention to how much we are straining the system, we will end up going faster but producing less, which is not only a waste of time and energy, it creates more issues for us to deal with. Issues that actually produce overall "drag" on the organization.

~ Drag ~

Inertia, or the absence of drag, is critical to high performance. There are two types of drag - physical nature and man-made. Let's go back to the race car analogy. The physical nature in that example is the atmosphere, specifically gravity. We can't do anything about that. In business, examples of physical drag are hours in the day, or perhaps the number of people you can employ. It may even be limitations of machinery and/or systems. These are things that are present that you have to work within.

Man-made drag in the racecar analogy is how the driver actually drives the car, how hard he brakes, how high he revs the engine before shifting, etc. All man-made drag; drag that is dependent upon human tendencies and desires.

In business, I define drag as "energy spent on anything other than achieving the mission or goal of the organization." This type of man-made drag may manifest in inefficient processes. Or perhaps it's training needs or people in the wrong seats. But the most destructive man-made drag comes in the form of gossip. It's the infamous sub-culture. It's not just the kind of petty, around the water cooler gossip. Things like what people wear, their hairstyle, their political views, etc., that's just petty gossip. It's still corrosive. It's not something you want to tolerate. It's still *drag*. But it's not the type that leaders wake up in the middle of the night thinking about. The most destructive is the type of gossip that undermines the mission and the "Who We Are" within the organization. It tends to directly attack Leadership in one form or another. It may manifest in gossip about the leader's abilities, poor decisions, and perceived weak work habits. This type of gossip has the potential of having serious disruption with real consequences to performance. This is where people spend a significant time undermining current efforts, policies, and processes. This eats away at the high productive culture you are working so hard to build and maintain.

~ The Baffled Co-Worker ~

Joan couldn't understand it. "How could 'Peggy' keep getting promoted? What does she have on upper management?" Joan proclaimed. Peggy had been there a good while. She was a hard worker, but continually rubbed people the wrong way. The people that worked around her were shocked with her first promotion to Supervisor, but when she was tapped to lead a new initiative and eventually became the Manager of that function, they were dumbfounded.

Over the years, Peggy's direct supervisor and the other leaders of the organization became aware of the stress and upheaval that her behavior caused, but didn't really do anything about it. A conversation here or there, talking other employees off the ledge, etc., but no real action in terms of improving Peggy's behavior.

A Regional VP went to the Sr. VP to describe how he had to go around behind Peggy, clean up, and explain-away the behavior and actions of Peggy every time her work intersected their areas of responsibility – but the response was always the same – "Peggy is loyal, her results are good. I'll talk to her." But nothing changed. She was allowed to "leave bodies in her wake" because of her results. The message was clear to the ranks – there are different rules and standards for some than others – the consequence of weak Leadership.

The irony of this situation is that the leader has the most ability to eliminate, or better yet, not create conflict in the first place. When I say create, I don't mean in an intentional way. I mean it is a consequence of how we are performing as a leader. As I referenced earlier, people are always watching you, the leader. They watch your work ethic. They watch to see if you are "practicing what you are preaching." How you handle stress, difficult conversations, customers, employees and others, this is what either feeds the positive sub-culture and rallies people around you, or has them further the destructive sub-culture of gossip.

I'm not suggesting that you spend all of your time trying to monitor or corral "gossip." I'm saying that if you work on "being" a leader that is worthy of someone following, you will eliminate the overwhelming majority of this type of "drag" before it ever happens. If you are working on "being" a leader worthy of following by Purpose, Impact, and Achievements – in that order – you are not only neutralizing what is really one of the hardest things to overcome, but you are actually replacing it with an environment of passionate pursuit of worthwhile goals. In other words, you are implementing Employee Engagement at an *inspired level.*

I've always loved the question, "If you were running into a burning building to save something or someone, would your people follow you?" I pray none of us will ever have to literally find this out. But the question is still valid. We obviously want people that will follow us into the burning building. To do this, we must be aware of our role in creating and sustaining all elements of Velocity – Direction *plus* Speed *minus* Drag.

~ Results, Results, Results – It's a huge component of the Discipline of Achievement ~

~ It's Why You are Here! ~

"It's why you are here!" John loved hearing this from the Sr. VP of Sales. It was the second quarter in a row where his team had exceeded their targets. He was riding the wave. He also remembered the conversations he had last year with the same VP when his team had missed their numbers two quarters in a row. That conversation was more like this, "John, what's the problem? You have a great territory, a full team, the same training and support, but you keep missing your numbers. This falls on you. Maybe you aren't right for the

position. You have to turn this around, and I mean now. We can't afford to keep carrying your territory. It's not fair to the rest of the company, and frankly, it's not acceptable. You are responsible. It's why you are here!"

In the prior vignette, the Sr. VP of Sales uses the same line, "It's why you are here!" Yet, a much different meaning comes from the line. This is where we must not confuse the syntax of Velocity Leadership with the level of importance placed upon each discipline. Let me be very clear; you will never be kept in a leadership position because of your style, your techniques, your personality, your team's following, your team's personal growth, or any other reason that doesn't include achieving or exceeding your results or goals. Never.

Business is about results. If you lead a youth group, it should be about results. If you lead a non-profit, it's about results. Regardless of what you run – big or small, one team or a company of teams – results matter. Results are what gives you, and more importantly, KEEPS you in a position to lead; it's your Seat at the Table.

Employee Engagement
World's Best vs. U.S. Organizations
Source: Gallup - State of the American Workplace 2017

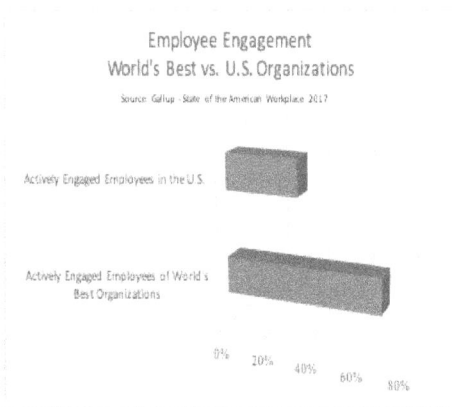

Actively Engaged Employees in the U.S.

Actively Engaged Employees of World's Best Organizations

0%   20%   40%   60%   80%

The key difference is that Bold Leaders understand that the results are just that — they are the scoreboard. They represent a by-product of Purpose and Impact. In fact, they are also a by-product of certain types of Achievements. But be clear, you never really get hired or put into a position of leadership to "develop your people." Companies are fine with that as long as you add, "Develop your people *and achieve your goals, hit your numbers, and grow your market to expectations.*" The "and" is the key for you to keep yourself in a position of having that kind of impact on people. In fact, Bold Leaders understand that developing others is the only way to sustainably hit the metrics they are judged upon.

You can have all kinds of achievements that aren't actually measurable results. You can turn a talented misfit into a producing machine. You can take someone with a great attitude but poor skills into a solid performer that may end up training others. You can take mediocre training and turn it into a world-class system. All of these are great achievements. But if you don't hit your numbers, you'll lose your Seat at the Table. Even though the previous achievements are great for the individuals involved, the achievements must be directed towards results. Period.

To relate this back to the story of "It's why you are here," the Sr. VP in that story seems to come off as someone who doesn't care about people, only numbers. But in reality, from a business standpoint, the VP is correct. It is "why you are here." It's your role in the organization. Also, keep in mind, it's why the Sr. VP is there also. He's answering to someone as well who is expecting results.

Keep in mind that from a business standpoint, results are why you are there. But when leading people, understand that is the "results why." The "operational why" is to serve those you lead, your clients and customers, and your co-workers. Your *Why* needs to be about people. Your results are just that… the results of how effective you are at leading others. This is why you must focus on your purpose first, then quickly transition your *Why* into having impact on those you lead and those around you. Then your achievements in those areas will end up with positive results. Results that will keep your *Seat at the Table*.

Direct your Disciplines of *Purpose* and *Impact* towards *Achieving* the results laid out in front of you…

It's why you are here!

Chapter 7

Discipline 3 - *Achievement*
The Tools You Need

If we truly adopt the 3 Disciplines of Velocity Leadership – Purpose, Impact & Achievements – we understand that we must embrace our need to continually get better at motivating, coaching, and navigating a myriad of personalities and situations. It's a very fluid way of being. It's not a "one and done" or a "fire and forget" type of thing. It's more like observe, assess, act, observe, assess, act… over and over again. Having said that, it's not like you are just wandering aimlessly in a sea of actions and reactions. There are tools that you can use to help navigate the seas of diversity and uniqueness that is leadership.

I use the term "tool" specifically and knowingly. You could substitute "tactic" or "technique." But tool is definitely more literal. Think of it this way. If you were given a new tool for work around the house, it would take a while to really get the "art" of using that tool. How hard do I push? What angle does it work best? How can I prep the area for the tool to work it's best? Add to this the fact that you've NEVER used it before. This is the same with many of the tools I'll be covering in this chapter. At first, it will be a little awkward. You'll have to learn the best way to use it. It will, at first, be a little clunky. You'll learn the best way to prep the environment and yourself to maximize its effectiveness.

You'll have to learn when to finesse and when to apply more pressure. You'll have to learn the difference in technique based upon the "material" you are working with (In the human realm, it's experience, personality, gender, generation, etc.) The bottom line is for these tools to work best for you, you have to use them. Get used to them. Learn constantly. Adapt. Adjust. To borrow from the U.S. Marine Corps: Improvise, Adapt, Overcome. If you do this with these tools and put them into the syntax of Velocity Leadership, you will be a leader worthy of following.

~ The 3 C's - Communication, Consistency, & Coaching ~

There are several factors that are present in all high-performing teams and organizations. Brendon Burchard[vii] has broken this down into 5 Qualities of High Performance – Clarity, Energy, Courage, Productivity, and Influence.

I believe that the first quality, Clarity, is in many ways the most important. All of the other qualities are subservient to Clarity. Without this, we can have lots of energy and courage, but towards what end? Productive towards what end? Our influence is used towards what end? Clarity – it's the key.

Chapter 7

~ Where are we going? ~

"I can't understand it, Kelly. We have all been here before. We are ready to accelerate. But we can't get a clear answer of where we are going or how we want to get there. Where's the leadership!?!" Sharon, the CFO, was clearly frustrated.

She is a seasoned veteran and very experienced in taking organizations to the maximum value. She's an outstanding CFO – one of the best I've ever met. But even with her experience and vision she, too, is languishing because of a lack of clarity.

My advice, "Sharon, you need to have a difficult conversation with your President and voice your concerns. Let him know from a fact-based position that we aren't getting what is possible in terms of growth because of the lack of clarity on direction and speed. We can't attain the velocity necessary to maximize the potential of the company if we don't have this."

The real question at this point is whether or not the President is a bold leader.

The scenario above is not really that uncommon. Even with highly-paid, experienced, and talented people, having and maintaining clarity of direction (mission) and speed (strategy) is a real struggle. At the speed of business today and shifting landscapes, we are all challenged to maintain clarity around our goals, our strategy, our mission, etc. If it's hard at that level of the organization, just imagine what it must be like in the ranks of the organization. This is where the "3 C's" come into play.

The 3 C's stand for Communication, Consistency, and Coaching. I first wrote about this in a book I published in 2004 – The No-nonsense Guide to Management Effectiveness. When it comes to the 3 C's, I've experienced them, or lack thereof, as an employee, a frontline manager, an executive leader and as the principal in an organization. I've been on all sides of this.

The power of the 3 C's is how they interact or work in tandem. You have to communicate the important things, the right things, consistently. By doing this, you will discover opportunities for coaching. Then you must take those opportunities to coach consistently and effectively, i.e., communicate. This symbiotic relationship is a flow in a non-linear fashion. It's more like liquids flowing and mixing together in a constant swirl. They intertwine in a very fluid and dynamic manner. The syntax is not the key. The relationship between the 3 is the key driver. Utilize them when they are needed to have the greatest impact. They are separate in terms of thought, interdependent in terms of effectiveness.

In the last 20 years or so, I've also observed the positive power of this when implemented and the destruction of it when neglected. In reality, this combination of traits is required in all 3 disciplines.

Chapter 7

~ Communication ~

There is no shortage of books and training on communication. In many ways, this book is all about communication. You can't lead if you can't communicate. This doesn't mean you have to be an extraordinary orator. It means you have to be constantly growing in your communication effectiveness. Also, you can't influence if you can't communicate on some level. Your purpose will have no power over yourself or others if you can't communicate it. You can't have impact on others if you can't communicate. And you certainly will not achieve the results you are looking for if you can't communicate with them. As you'll see, it's a critical factor in the power of leading by embracing the 3 C's.

Communication is not a static skill. It's not once you have it, you are set, finished, checked the box. It's an evolutionary skill. Why? Because what we are communicating, and more importantly, who we are communicating to, is always changing. It changes quickly. Sometimes it requires a shift in direction, which means we have to adjust what we are communicating. Again, this is happening at a seemingly frenetic pace. When it comes to communicating, it's important that we embrace the fact that we must be focused on improvement in this area daily.

Communication, in terms of the 3 C's, is all about being open. It's about sharing where we are going and why. Think of it in terms of over-communicating. The reason I say this is because that's how it feels when you are doing it.

You'll say something to yourself like, "I don't have time to continually go back and explain why I'm asking for every single thing." Or, "It's not possible. After all, how many times should I have to keep telling people why we are doing something or why something changed?" The list can go on, but you get my drift here. The key here is effectiveness. If you could have your people be more effective by some meaningful multiple, say 10%, 15%, 20% - would it be worth it? Would it be worth the pain of over-communicating? If it was that effective, how could it be called "over" communicating? This is where you want to check yourself. Does it feel like it's over-communicating because it is that, or because you just don't want to keep having the same conversations over and over? In other words, what feels like over-communication is really us thinking some version of "They should have already gotten this." Or, "They don't need to know this." Or, "I'm so tired of having to always explain things to this detail." Or a myriad of other thoughts that show up telling us that this isn't worth it or it's not necessary.

~ The Early Riser ~

"Mike comes into my office every morning at about 7:15 and wants to talk. He chit-chats, talking about this and that. He'll throw in a few thoughts around prospects or sales approaches. But for the most part, I feel like the guy is just asking me to validate him. Tell him he's good enough. That he has 'leadership potential.' I don't know. The guy's just a pain in

my keister. I come in early to get work done before everyone shows up and I'm spending my time coddling one guy. It's just doesn't seem worth it," a Regional Sales Director (This was your humble author by the way! Yikes!) speaking to his boss, the Sr. VP of Sales. The VP responded, "Not sure it's worth it, huh? What if that's what it takes for Mike to hit his numbers every month? Month in, month out. Would it be worth it then?" Checkmate. End of conversation. I think I muttered something like, "Good point. Gotta go."

The "Early Riser" story is a great example of how we "feel" like something's not worth it – that it is over-communicating – but in reality, if that is what it takes to achieve your goals, IT'S WORTH IT! I also love the fact that I actually said, "I come in to get work done." Uh, Kelly, what work would that be that is so much more important than having an *impact* on one of your people so they could *achieve* their goals? It sounds like I need to have a little talk with myself about priorities and the syntax of being a BOLD Leader!

A simple tool that I use to help me gauge communication is: Observe, Assess, Act, Repeat. In this example, when I observe myself having thoughts of "this is a waste of time," I want to assess that. It's quick and simple, "Why would Mike need this? What am I not providing that gives him the confidence to move forward without these conversations, or at least the frequency of them? Then act.

This is where coaching would come into play. Then I observe. What affect did the coaching have? Is it better, worse, no change? What could I do differently to have more impact? Then act!

The simple thought process of Observe, Assess, Act, Repeat is a great way to move forward with consistency.

~ Consistency ~

The relationship of Consistency is multi-faceted in terms of the 3 C's. It's about being consistent with your level of communication. It's about taking advantage of the coaching moments when they occur in the course of your day with your people. It's also about who you are "Being" throughout the days, weeks, and months. In some ways, this is the most important because "being" implies certain behaviors. Behaviors being defined as the way one conducts themselves, especially toward others. Another word for this is deportment. Deportment meaning a person's behaviors or mannerisms.

Bold Leadership encompasses both, how you behave and who you are being while exhibiting that behavior. Let me say it this way – it's not enough to just do or behave in the right way. You have to do it in a way that is genuine, compassionate and authentic. Do you remember earlier in the book when I said, "Your *being* is what gives your words influence and power"? This is part of the consistency that I'm talking about in relation to the 3 C's. By being consistent, you create a consistent environment which is critical for us to achieve maximum velocity. It's all about avoiding the dreaded self-imposed *drag* we spoke about earlier. To reiterate, there is enough drag being applied to us from outside influences, influences we have no say in, that we need to eliminate this type of drag being created and perpetuated by ourselves.

~ Morning Coffee ~

Driving in to work my mind was drifting from one to-do item to the other. I kept trying to focus on how I could be more impactful in those situations and what I really needed to develop. But this nagging thought kept coming to my mind, pulling me away from focusing on my work. "Coffee, coffee, the smell of coffee." This wasn't some need or urge on my part. It wasn't about me needing a jolt of caffeine. It was my boss.

To set the stage, I was usually the first in the office. I liked getting there early to have some quiet time. The only rival to that was my boss. If I wasn't the first to arrive, he was. But here's the kicker. When he arrived that early, it was usually for a reason – not a good reason. Not that he would necessarily be upset or concerned with me, but he would be upset about something. This meant that everyone would feel it. He wasn't going to be bringing his

"A" game; he was going to be bringing his "agitated" game.

So what does this have to do with coffee? My telltale sign that he was in the office was the smell of coffee. The first to arrive almost always made the coffee. If he arrived and there was no coffee made, he always made it. I would walk into the office and always take a big whiff hoping to not smell the coffee. It was such a big deal that I was thinking of it on my way to work.

You might be thinking, so what's the big deal about a boss being agitated? Everyone has to endure this from time-to-time, right? It's not about his or her demeanor for the day.

It's about the fact that the inconsistency of behavior and environment took energy away from me working on how I could improve or accomplish the mission to wondering which boss was going to show up. This is classic "drag" – meaning it diverts energy to something other than accomplishing the goal or achieving the mission.

This consistency shows up on many other levels. As part of implementing the Velocity Leadership System and our Executive Coaching Programs, consistency is addressed from many different angles. But it all comes down to the same thing. Being consistent in who we are being, enhances our activities in terms of communication and coaching. It also sets the tone for others to maximize their growth and ultimately their performance.

~ Coaching ~

When was the last time that you felt like you really dug in with someone to show them a way or process that really had a life-altering impact on them? I'm not sure how fast I could come up with one of these times. But if I take a moment and think, I can come up with several. Part of it is the nature of my work. It's my role to help people have those little epiphanies that lead them to marked improvement and growth. But if you think about it, is it any different for you? If you are a leader, you help people grow. If you are a Bold Leader, you have it in your DNA to have a meaningful, positive impact on someone. Without this, you have no way of keeping your Seat at the Table. You can't achieve goals consistently over the long haul if you don't have impact on your people in a way that catapults them forward.

Because of this, you must think of yourself as a coach. You must be looking for those times where you can coach *in the work*. This brings us to an integral component to Velocity Leadership. To have any training, culture development, and employee development actually stick, you have to keep it "*in the work.*" Let me give you the most blatant example of this, and then I'll relate it back to Coaching within the 3 C's context.

Have you ever gone into a lobby of an organization and seen a mission statement framed or a plaque up on the wall? Most organizations of any size have this type of thing. It's usually worded very cleverly. It sounds good. It looks good. Reading it all by itself is usually inspiring. But here's the rub. If you then go to random employees and ask them the company's mission statement, virtually none of them can repeat it, let alone live it. Don't get me wrong, there are some companies where that will not happen. People will know them, and they will embrace them. Chick-fil-a is a great example of this. The overwhelming majority of organizations will fall in the former category, not the latter.

The reason for this is that there is no integration of the statement to the work that people do every day. We have to get the mission statement off the wall and into the work. It must become a lens through which people work. When you do this, it starts to affect how people make decisions, align priorities, and work together. To relate this back to Coaching, we must coach with a common purpose. By doing this, we utilize the power of the *Objective 3rd Party*, which is what I'll be diving into next. In short, you have a reason that is bigger than you or the person you are coaching to be doing the coaching in the first place. It changes how you coach and it changes how someone receives coaching.

Coaching in the 3 C's is to coach "in the work" and to do it in a way that supports a bigger cause – something bigger than ourselves! Sound familiar? The 3 C's - Communication, Consistency, and Coaching gives you a framework for interacting with your people in a way that eliminates drag and feeds the necessary discipline of *Impact*.

Chapter 7

~ Objective 3rd Party ~

One of the strong attributes of the Velocity Leadership system is the creation of an effective "*Who We Are.*" Simply put, this is how people operate and who they are being on a day-to-day, moment-by-moment basis. It's the standard with which we gauge ourselves and others. It's a reminder of Why we are doing what we are doing and how to effectively be who we need to be to achieve that in excellence. Again, it's the organization's self-imposed standard. It's a benchmark of being. By having a strong and meaningful *Who We Are,* it becomes larger than any one person. Any person. Let me give you an example of how this works in having *impact* on others in a meaningful way. If Joe is part of your team and he is taking shortcuts or not doing a piece of the process, you can address it with the Objective 3rd Party. It goes something like this:

"Joe, we all agreed that the best way to handle this type of customer concession (or "x" - you fill in the blank) issue is to follow-up with an email alerting our client support group so they can proactively reach out and follow-up. We've had repeated instances where you haven't done this. We've talked about it before, but you keep skipping this step. Joe, that's just not Who We Are."

Pause right there. When you said, "that's not *Who We Are,*" that's the Objective 3rd Party. It immediately takes the conversation from being "you versus them" to "Who We Are" calling him out. This subtle difference does two things. It takes some of the personal, forehead-to-forehead confrontation out of it. Additionally, it re-engages a higher call to action. It reminds them we are doing this because of something bigger than ourselves. It brings the full weight of the collective to the situation rather than a 'me versus him' scenario. This eliminates much, if not all, of the excuses and rationalizations that come from someone who is repeatedly doing the wrong thing.

The Objective 3rd Party also has a huge impact on the opposite situation. It gives more impact to the recognition of good behavior. When you see someone stepping up, going the extra mile, doing the right thing, being the behaviors and attitude you have set out, you can literally say, "Great job Ellen, that's *Who We Are.*" In this case, the Objective 3rd Party gives more weight and meaning to the recognition. It's a beautiful thing.

Actually, saying the words "*Who We Are*" is a critical component to keeping a higher standard and a compelling vision alive and "in the work." When we roll-out the Vision and the *Who We Are* to the organization, we are looking for people to identify with it and engage in it while doing their work. This is the beginning of the "in the work" mentality. It is not some cheerleader type of thing, but a meaningful way of getting mission, vision, and values off of the wall and onto the desk. It is not just a wallpaper on their computer or a printout pinned to a cubicle, but something that they use to make decisions, to have meaningful dialogue, and to challenge them to better performance and new heights.

As we work into the organization, I challenge people to say to others "that's *Who We Are*" or "that's NOT *Who We Are.*" It's always humorous because some people have such a hard time with this. I get it. Asking someone with introverted tendencies to say "that's *Who We Are*" to someone privately, let alone in a more public setting where others can hear it, is awkward at best. Perhaps even embarrassing. But what we've found is that in pretty short order people are saying it with a different tenor. I've overheard them saying those words to customers, to partners, to others in the organization in very deliberate tones. It starts to take on a life of its own – a life bigger than any one person. This is when I know we have crossed a great divide in this journey, through one valley, scaled a mountain, and now looking at the landscape from a different vantage point. It's really a cultural milestone to high performance.

The *Who We Are* raises the bar for everyone when we keep it in the work. It starts to mean something in terms of how and why we do our work. Ultimately it becomes the Objective 3rd Party that challenges everyone to rise to the occasion. To create and implement this full-on High Productivity Culture Program is a very involved process that takes commitment from leadership. But you can use this one tool for your department or team. It's obviously most effective if the entire organization is part of it, but it still reaps huge rewards in leading your people on the pursuit of excellence at any level of an organization.

~ *Clarity Re-visited* ~

I'm going to be touching on more tools in the coming chapters, but I wanted to bring this chapter back to where we began, Clarity.

Chapter 7

Clarity of purpose. Clarity of mission. Clarity of path or strategy. Clarity of *Why*. The effectiveness of any tool is in direct proportion to the clarity surrounding it. Many times we go to seminars or read books and learn really great techniques and tactics. We try to implement them and find that they aren't as effective as we'd hoped or maybe not effective at all. So we stop. We chalk it up as "That won't work here," or "That won't work for me." I've found that this happens for a few consistent reasons.

First, is just that – consistency. We don't implement a tool consistently for a long enough period of time for it to work. We can get better at implementing it by being consistent. Our people will have a chance to change or adapt to it in a positive way if we do it consistently. In other words, they respond better as they get used to it. If we are going to attempt something new, we have to stick with it to give our people and ourselves time to reap the benefit of it.

Second, we don't really implement it with confidence. We go in with a "we'll try it" attitude but with no real commitment. When we do this, our people know it. It comes across like a "flavor of the month" type of thing, so they are fine with just waiting it out or "weathering the storm." It will soon pass, and they can go back to "normal." If you are going to attempt something, you need to do it with the expectation and commitment that it's going to work and it's going to help us all perform better.

Finally, we try to implement techniques into an environment that lacks clarity. We are back to clarity again. I point this out to be redundant and to illustrate how a lack of clarity can infiltrate your organization at so many levels.

I'll leave it with this:

Take ownership of clarity irrespective of where you are inside the organization. This shows up as you making sure there is no lack of clarity in how you express where you are going and why. This is your role as a leader. If you are at the top, there is no excuse. It's your responsibility and you must own it.

If you are somewhere in the middle of the organization and start to express clarity, it will be noticed and it will give you the platform to begin to seek clarity from upstream. If you are a frontline worker with no management responsibilities, you can express clarity to customers and to co-workers. Your actions will give a tangible definition to the term "leaders at all levels."

I remember one time when I said to someone that I was "fairly certain" about something and they busted out laughing. In fact, that is a ridiculous statement. When it comes to leadership, being "fairly clear" or "pretty clear" about where we are going, how we are going to get there, and why it's important to our customers, employees, and the world at large... is unacceptable. If you want to be a Bold Leader, a leader that is respected and accomplished, you demand this clarity and realize that all paths to excellence begin with it.

For any tool to truly have a lasting impact on productivity, it must be surrounded with clarity and the commitment to see it through.

Chapter 7

<u>Chapter 8</u>

Employee Engagement
It's Not About the Employee

~ The Case for Employee Engagement ~

If we are going to be Bold Leaders, we have to address the issue of Employee Engagement. It's a hot topic and has been for several years. But we have to shift our perspective on this if we are truly going to have a strong impact on those around us to achieve the results we are seeking.

It's widely understood that perks are not the same as true employee engagement effort. Perks are definitely a factor, but in reality, they are a secondary tool to the true focus of employee engagement. No amount of gym memberships, flex time, profit-sharing, or any other perk, unique or not, can trump the positive effect of having people believe, and feel, that their work has importance and meaning beyond the bottom-line. This is one of the key drivers to employee engagement.

Another important note about employee engagement is that, in very real terms, it's a key driver to having a competitive advantage today. In fact, I believe it's one of the last true bastions of true, unique, competitive advantage. Here's why.

Chapter 8

More than ever in history we live in a time where there are virtually no secrets. Products are being knocked-off at record pace. Systems are being copied. Any time there is success in a segment, people put their eyes on it and, soon to follow, their investment in copying it. I'm not suggesting that there aren't patents that can be defended or exclusives that can't exist. But clearly, our ability to protect uniqueness is becoming more difficult by the second.

But if we can create an environment, a culture of employee engagement where people feel they are part of something bigger than themselves and something that matters to them, then they want to contribute to it. Help them know their contribution matters. This type of culture creates a unique competitive advantage.

If you are competing and everything else is the same, your ability to engage your employees is *the key* competitive advantage. It's so unique that even if one of your people leaves to go to a competitor or start their own competitive company *and* they go through the same steps to create a culture of engagement, it still isn't the culture you created in your own organization. Your culture is still unique, and because of this, no one can steal it, knock it off, or copy it. It's impossible. If you couple this uniqueness factor with the overwhelming evidence of productivity improvement through engagement – you can compete with anyone and ultimately, become all that you want to be within your respected department, organization, or industry, for that matter.

Only 33% of Employees are Actively Engaged

Employees Actively Engaged

Employees Actively Disengaged

Employees Not Engaged

0%　10%　20%　30%　40%　50%　60%

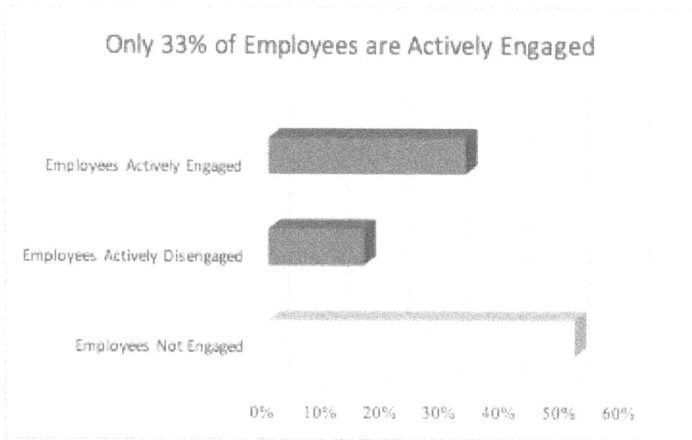

But if employee engagement is so effective and critical to the bottom-line performance of organizations, why do so many employee engagement programs fail to achieve the desired results?

~ It's Not Really About the Employee ~

Here's the real rub with employee engagement. We have a tendency to believe that it's really about the employee. We measure the success of these types of initiatives around the employee. It's a valid measurement, but just like the entire thinking around Velocity Leadership, by the time you get to the results, it's a scorecard. We then tend to also blame the employees or the HR department for the lack of effectiveness. The reality is, just like virtually everything else in your organization, this is about leadership.

If you have a great employee engagement program, but leadership is not modeling it, referring to it, living it, actually being it... it fails. Or at the very least, the effectiveness is mitigated dramatically. Most times it just flat-out fails. Results aren't what we expected. The time it takes to implement doesn't seem to have the rewards we were looking for. It doesn't seem worth the investment.

The "reasons" to stop are overwhelming. Then we get finance involved and they are eager to remove that program from the expense side of the house. They can easily add this all back to the bottom line in next year's projections. Thus, the program dies. And in many cases, the engagement is now worse than before we embarked on the program in the first place.

There are a couple of reasons that these types of initiatives fail. It's usually a combination of factors, but here are the few that I've found to be consistent.

1) It is viewed and communicated as an HR initiative.

I love my HR folks. I work closely with lots of them in my work and have come to grow close to many on a personal and professional level. I have a lot of respect for them. But in all honesty, there is a constant struggle to have HR viewed on par with other business units internally. I won't go into all of the factors for this at this time, but programs rolled out under the moniker of an "HR Initiative" definitely impacts the way they are "viewed." There are ways to change this, but that's for a different time.

The real takeaway here is that any employee engagement program that you launch should be about achieving business metrics and goals. Why? Because that's what it is. Bold Leaders recognize this because it is specifically aligned with the Disciplines of *Purpose & Impact*. Why are we leading? Why is our company in existence? How can I have a meaningful impact on those I lead? How can I help them do the same with those they lead or work with? These questions and answers directly relate to why this is a business initiative, not an HR initiative. Search for them. Apply them to this type of initiative. It is one of the keys to success.

2) Lack of Clarity in Purpose

Typically, these programs involve some sort of survey, then assessment of results, then action plan, then roll out, etc. All the time this is happening, vague or unclear reasoning is given to the employee as to what we are doing and why. This is a classic *lack of communication*. The communication plan for this type of endeavor is equally important to the plan itself. In fact, if we roll this out effectively, we start increasing the engagement level of our employees immediately. Granted, some of this engagement is skepticism, perhaps even cynicism. But the benefit is that

THREE STEPS TO CRAFTING AN EMPLOYEE VALUE PROPOSITION

1. Clarify your organization's identity.
2. Study your best employees.
3. Create compelling messaging.

Source: Gallup – State of the American Workplace 2017

we are having our employees consciously think about why we are doing what we are doing, how we can do it better, how we want to involve them in this conversation, etc. This level of communication is a leadership thing. In fact, it's a Bold Leadership activity.

3) Unclear Next Steps for Management

It's one thing to have a coherent and clear purpose from inside the executive suite. It's another to have this clarity of purpose and next steps for those who are responsible to keep it going in a positive direction. This is management within the ranks. Whether it's at the Director, Manager, or Supervisor level within the organization, clear next steps are critical. Once again, this is a leadership thing. It relates back to spending as much time on the communication and rollout plans as the plan itself.

Keeping it "in the work" is a critical component to any engagement program that is intended to impact sustainable productivity. (Sidebar here – if that's not its purpose, you shouldn't do it.) What are the ways we are going to speak about the program in terms of the work that is already being done? How are we going to have it live on the desk of our employees versus on the wall or in a Slack channel or on the shared drive? These key understandings and activities are critical to the success of this type of initiative.

Clear communication and involvement of frontline management are critical for this project to sustain itself past the "Remember when we tried X" stage.

4) Too much focus on "doing" versus "being."

There is no doubt that this type of initiative will alter how we are doing things within the organization. But that is not the goal of engagement. The goal of engagement is to have our employees go from what they can receive from the organization to what they can contribute to the organization. This can only happen if we have that contribution be about something that matters to the employee.

Employees may start out with the mindset of, "What can I receive from the company?" (Pay, perks, education). But we need to transcend this to, "What can I give to the cause?" (The reason we are in business in the first place). This can only happen if we focus on "being." This engages the core of our employees. It resides through their brain or intellect into their heart or emotion. This is the human side of the equation. It touches upon the innate desire to be part of something bigger than ourselves.

~ *Employee Engagement is really about Leadership Engagement* ~

In the land of sustainable growth, there is a big spotlight on employee engagement. It's warranted. It's definitely one of the pillars of success. As Marcus Lemonis[viii] points out in his highly successful TV show, *The Profit*, it's about Product, Process, and People. Employee engagement is directly focused on People first. Then they can do amazing things with the process, and perhaps even with the product.

There have been many studies that illustrate the positive impact on business results of companies that are more engaged within the employee ranks. These are not categorized in the ranks of soft-skills, but of hard, tangible numbers that show up on P&L's and balance sheets. Having engaged employees is a needle mover.

But we have to recognize the fact that if we, as leaders don't give the same level of importance and impact on employee engagement as a unique competitive advantage as we might a marketing plan or sales goals or market share growth, then we are undermining the ability of this type of plan to work in the first place.

When was the last time you spoke about your level of employee engagement in your standard meetings that cover sales, attrition and other strategic initiatives? Most leaders don't have a resounding positive answer to this. Don't despair. You are far from alone. But if we are going to take on this mission of eradicating weak leadership, we have to be willing to start with ourselves, in our organization. This is what Bold Leadership is all about.

When was the last time that any innovative and work-intense initiative in your organization actually provided the results you were looking for, if you weren't solidly committed to them? Let me answer for you: most likely NEVER. There are always exceptions, but rarely.

Employee engagement starts with Leadership engagement. There is no way around it. This means that Leadership must model the behavior we are looking for from our employees. We must utilize the speak, we must utilize the lens, we must utilize the engagement tools we are presenting and requesting our employees use first… and last… and in-between.

When we think about our organization – where we want it to go, how we want it to be – we have to embrace the fact that the level of true engagement of our employees is a critical factor. In fact, it is THE critical factor if we are going to achieve the growth we are looking for in a sustainable manner. We need to do our part in a competitive world to be a place where high-quality people want to work. This doesn't happen by chance any more than a marketing plan just appears. It's something you have to focus on and work on consistently.

This is at the core of Bold Leadership. By focusing on our purpose for being a leader and transitioning that into action of having lasting, positive impact for those we lead and work with, we are creating the environment, and more importantly, the skillsets, to achieve desired results in a consistent manner. This is not to say that there is no ownership with the employee at large. It absolutely has to do with their ownership. But their ownership is in large part dependent upon the leader's commitment and engagement in the first place.

This is why I say it's not about Employee Engagement. It's about Leadership Engagement – *Bold Leadership Engagement!*

Chapter 8

~ Keeping It in the Work ~

This theme of *Keeping It in the Work* is a resounding theme. For leadership to be effective in a developmental and/or result-oriented way, we have to keep concepts of growth "in the work," meaning relatable to daily tasks for our employees.

This is the challenge with having development and training being an "add-on" to the work. It manifests like this: We decide that we need communication training for our customer service group. So what do we do? We ask HR to look for some training company or something online that we can use. Makes sense.

Then we find something that passes our vetting process and we decide to send people somewhere or have someone come in to train. This is a half-day or day-long event. They get some good stuff. They have some fun, which ups their energy for a day or two. It's really a good thing. And then, we throw them back into their cubicle, and the reality of work comes back to the forefront, and within a few days, they resort to old habits.

Then we look back on the training in a few months and determine that it wasn't very good. It didn't really change anything. We could've saved the money and time. We might still say it was good because they got some time together and it helped break the monotony of work. But is this real performance change? Not really.

Here's why: we didn't do anything to transition this to their work. We didn't have follow-up conversations to talk about how they were implementing their new learnings. This is a critical step, and it's important to any type of training or cultural initiative.

Many times, the stress and speed of work will tug on our employees' ability to implement new thinking and functional methods of doing their work. This ties right into employee engagement. As I said earlier, effective employee engagement results in employees thinking more about what they can contribute to a meaningful cause rather than what they can get from the company. It's the classic, "what can I give" versus "what can I get" thinking.

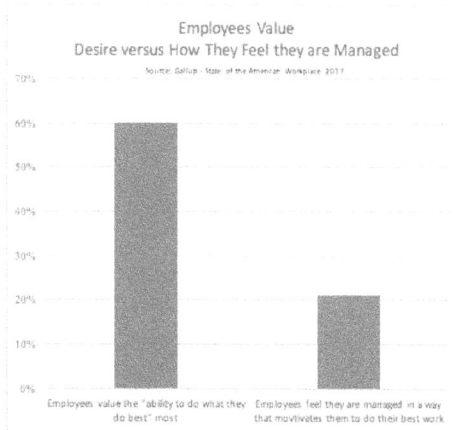

Employees Value
Desire versus How They Feel they are Managed
Source: Gallup - State of the American Workplace 2017

This is why we must make sure that we get our "who we want to be" out of the training manual, out of the slide presentation, and off of the wall of our lobby.

Bold Leaders understand that the key to having consistent positive change for our people, whether it's cultural or task-oriented, is to keep the change or desired behaviors *in the work*.

Chapter 8

<u>Chapter 9</u>

Bold Leadership
Putting It All Together

The title of this chapter might suggest to you that I'm going to now spell all of this out with exact step-by-step instruction. It's not my intention to mislead you. But it is my intention to challenge your typical thought process. If I were to give you a step-by-step manual or map, I'd be feeding into the typical trap of "tell me what to do." Bold Leaders are built around who they are being first. Their "doing" comes from their "being." This means we'll be building Bold Leadership qualities into our presence, so we can continuously adapt our tactics and skills.

If we are going to eradicate weak leadership, we have to build ourselves and other leaders from the inside-out. To do this, we'll have to adopt a few basics that allow us to put all of the pieces together in a cohesive and effective way.

I'm going to describe 9 perspectives and ways of being that tie Purpose, Impact and Achievement together from an inside-out approach. This is effectively the DNA of a Bold Leader.

Chapter 9

~ Nine Attributes of a Bold Leader ~

1) Embodying Ownership over Responsibility – Bold Leaders realize that it's one thing to find out who's responsible and another to cultivate or embrace ownership. Too often we look for the responsible party, especially when something has gone wrong. We must shift our thinking to forward-looking versus backward investigating. By owning the situation, we immediately activate the vision of what we are going to do moving forward. Once we've established this and have rallied those around us, we will still go back to look at who and what was responsible, but we'll be doing it from a coaching and development mindset. This puts us back into the leadership role versus the judge and jury role. As the Leader, it is your ownership that will move you and your team forward. By modeling this behavior, you'll be fostering ownership in those you lead.

2) Legacy of Value – Bold Leaders seek to have a legacy of adding significant value to all they lead and are associated with. By doing this, they don't rely on results to establish their worth, but by the results of those they touched. This is a meaningful legacy that surpasses any form of awards, plaques, monetary gains, etc. This is about having a legacy of "human currency." This is the true payoff for Bold Leaders. Although it's true that if you do this, you'll most likely have all kinds of material gains in your life, that's just a by-product of the goal. A legacy of value is what really drives Bold Leaders.

3) Future Vision – Bold Leaders consistently tie current behaviors and needs to future outcomes. We understand that having people associate their work with a meaningful cause is key to a high performance and the pursuit of excellence. It's what fosters creativity within our ranks and has people want to give more than just receive. Future vision is inspiring through the meaning of their work versus just a milestone to achieve. Milestones, KPI's, MBO's and Goals are all important tools for excellence, but Bold Leaders understand that the meaning of the journey is what will propel us all to the achievement of those goals.

4) Worthy of Following – There is a lot that goes into being worthy of following – integrity, compassion, positive values, belief in the human capacity to grow and overcome. The list can go on. Bold Leaders embrace the challenge of being worthy of following by pouring into their people. They are undaunted in this approach. They demand more from their people from the position of compassionate expectation. They see in their people what they may not be able to see in themselves and relentlessly pursue ways of pulling it out of them in a way that is rewarding to the follower. It's about supporting the positive growth of those they lead and associate with.

5) Inspiring – There is no doubt that Bold Leaders are inspiring. But they don't all go about this the same way. Some may be great motivators through their ability to communicate. Others may inspire through their vulnerability. Others, through their actions. For most, it is some combination of these and other methods. This is why Bold Leaders work on their "being" first. This allows them

to inspire in their own authentic and unique way. Bold Leaders aren't cookie-cutter leaders. They are authentic leaders that embrace the ways of becoming great leaders instead of just "doing" what they've been told works. This is what gives power to their doing and what inspires those around them to reach for new heights themselves.

6) Develop Allegiance – Followers of Bold Leaders will follow them into the "burning building." They build trust through authentic interactions and behaviors consistent with their words. They feel a kinship to those they lead and vice-versa. They are clear about hierarchy but respect the fact that we are all human. From that perspective, we are all brothers and sisters. This allows them to develop protocols and guidelines and even rules in a way that doesn't violate basic human respect. This is how they develop followers that will follow them into the burning building when the situation arises. This same type of respect also manifests in dealing with disagreement, poor communication, and abrupt changes in priorities and focus. It's a human bond that all Bold Leaders pursue.

7) Mirror First – When it comes to development, Bold Leaders always look in the mirror first. They look for ways that they can improve and ways that they can grow. They do this not just for their own good, but they know it's the only way they can continue to lead those around them. No one can lead others past their own ability to exemplify what they are demanding of others. They are on a continuous journey of growth and self-development. They look for ways to do this through books, seminars, and conferences, just like other leaders. But they also look for it from their people.

They understand that they can learn from everyone, including those they lead, and they aren't afraid to admit it. In fact, Bold Leaders verbalize this to instill this perspective into those they lead. It deepens the allegiance at a human level and creates the environment for others to "look in the mirror" as well.

8) Decisive – Bold Leaders take action. There's an old saying in business that there is more money lost and opportunity squandered from the lack of decision than that of wrong decisions. Bold Leaders are not afraid to fail. They realize that fear fosters inaction, which causes a loss in virtually every area of leadership development. The loss of confidence from their followers is too great to become timid and indecisive. If you want to be a Bold Leader, you have to be bold. They realize that it's not so much if you make a mistake, it's what you do when that happens that either propels you forward or yanks you backwards. Decisiveness is not an option.

9) Bold Leaders Win – The mindset of a Bold Leader is that they are going to win. The difference with Bold Leaders compared to others that hold this belief is that they don't view it as "winning at all costs." They operate as winning at all investments. Winning through investing in others is playing full out in the growth of those around them directed towards a common, worthwhile goal. Bold Leaders are very cognizant of the numbers, the metrics by which they are measured. They never lose sight of them and they don't allow their people to do so either. Their method might be slightly different than other "outcome-driven" leaders. It truly is the difference between cost and investment. Investing in the

growth of others. Investing in the growth of themselves. Focusing on who they are being while they are doing and passing that on to others is how they win. They win in legacy AND the scoreboard. They build organizations that are a force to be reckoned with.

Bold Leaders win, and they win for the right reasons.

Chapter 10

Velocity Leadership Challenge
Are You Willing?

I started this book with a request, a challenge, if you will. A challenge to join me on the mission to eradicate weak leadership. Are you willing to commit to that challenge? Are you willing to take the steps necessary to eradicate the weak leadership habits you've developed first? Are you ready to reorder everything you've ever been taught about leadership so you can adopt and embrace the Purpose, Impact, Achievement model of being a Bold Leader?

I know it's a lot to ask. I know it's not simple in light of all you have in front of you. But if not you, who? Who will do it? Should we all wait on others to forge our own trail? I don't think so. And if you made it this far in the book, I don't think you do either. None of us are alone in this. In fact, we have many more people primed and ready to join us than we know.

We are all tired of having our lives affected by weak leadership. I've met no one in my life who can't associate with the examples that I used at the beginning of this book. There are so many more examples of weak leadership that it's easy to find others who see it and agree with it. We've outlined the concrete facts around why this is worthy of your effort and commitment. Regardless where we are in life, whether we are leading entire companies, divisions,

113

departments, groups, or just our own families, the evidence submitted in this book from objective third parties, personal experiences of myself, and others, supplies plenty of evidence that there is a need and there's a better way.

For some who read this book, they may be saying, "I already do a lot of this." That wouldn't surprise me. But for you, my question would be, "What if you did all of it? What if you thought about your legacy in terms of the value you developed in others rather than just your own tangible achievements? What if?"

Velocity Leadership is a movement. It's a belief that there's a better way to be a leader because there's a better reason to become one. It's a belief that by tapping into an innate human desire we actually feed our souls while achieving our goals. We don't do it because of the cost of weak leadership. That's just the catalyst to start the work. We do it because of the cost of lost opportunities for us to gain meaning out of our own lives and the lives of those we lead and impact.

Velocity Leadership isn't a system or a gimmick. It's an authentic way of being. It stands for something bigger than ourselves. It stands for something that brings real value to our organizations by developing real value of our people. We are about transforming how we lead and manage others to a place of selfless giving. As my friend August Turak[ix] teaches, "It is in your own self-interest to forget your self-interest."

Velocity Leadership is about dying to self. It's about scratching the surface on the nagging question, "Why am I here?" What is my purpose?" You aren't going to get a full answer out of this, though you may very well get on the path to that answer.

To me, leadership is more than a role. It's a path; it's my path. It's a huge part of who I am. I struggle. I make mistakes. I let people down. I break some of my own rules. But I carry on. Sometimes I carry the guilt of my past. Sometimes I'm able to off-load the guilt by setting things right so that I can marshal on with exuberance and excitement and anticipation of things to come.

Velocity Leadership isn't about perfection. It's about the pursuit of excellence through the giving of all I have to support others on their journey, their growth path.

Velocity Leadership is far from being a robot of "doing." It's about being willing to step into leading in a human and authentic way. It's about being aware of who we are "being" while we are "doing." It's about observing, assessing, acting, and repeating that process over and over and over again. It's a consistent pursuit of growth and excellence.

Why do we do this? Because we are worthy of that pursuit. We are worthy of being followed because of who we are being for those around us. We know, deep in our hearts, that we don't have to settle, and our people don't have to settle either.

If we are going to truly eradicate weak leadership, we must first work on ourselves, so we can pour into others. This is the essence of Bold Leadership.

Are you ready to answer the call? Are you ready to answer *your* call? My faith has me believe that we all have a calling. Leading, or eradicating weak leadership, may or may not be the calling I'm speaking about. Perhaps this is a subset of it. Regardless, this is a very real need and if you've read this book this far, I believe you are in a position to address this need. In that sense, it's *your* calling.

Will you join me on my mission to eradicate weak leadership? Will you contribute to that cause by working on yourself, so you can create a legacy of growth and development in others? So that you can make a lasting impact and create a substantial legacy of meaning?

If so, do me this one last favor. Let me know. Go to VelocityLeadership.com and declare it, leave me a brief note as to why you are committed to being a Bold Leader. Your investment in the time to do this will be worth the effort. I promise.

Go be a leader, a Bold Leader. Your journey starts now!

Chapter 10

Chapter 10

About the Author

Kelly Castor is a leader's leader.

He's led at all levels in organizations and brings a unique perspective from his 30+ years of experience. He understands that leadership is not about degrees or trainings or talent, it's about people – their motivations, needs, and desires. It's about tapping into the true potential of people and directing them towards a common goal. It's about stretching beliefs and shattering fears. It's about bold application of proven fundamentals.

Kelly Castor is the founder of Velocity Leadership – a high-performance consulting organization that focuses on developing and engaging people towards a higher level of performance. Utilizing real-life experiences, Kelly has developed techniques and tools to tap into a higher level of human performance with consistency and sustainability.

From the C-Suite to Front-line Management, the tools and mindsets necessary for extraordinary success have been developed, implemented, and refined from an experiential level. Velocity Leadership isn't theoretical; it's practical, it's real, and it's effective.

Velocity Leadership: Direction *plus* Speed *minus* Drag!

Disclaimer & Copyright Information

Some of the events, details, and conversations have been recreated from memories. In order to maintain their anonymity, in some instances, the names of individuals and places have been changed. As such, some identifying characteristics and details may have changed.

Although the author and publisher have made every effort to ensure that the information in this book was correct at press time, the author and publisher do not assume and hereby disclaim any liability to any party for any loss, damage, or disruption caused by errors or omissions, whether such errors or omissions result from negligence, accident, or any other cause. The author is solely responsible for the content contained in this book.

Cover illustration, book design and production
Copyright © 2018 by Tribute Publishing LLC
www.TributePublishing.com

All quotes, unless otherwise noted,
are attributed to the respective author or to the Holy Bible.

Velocity Leadership

[i] Simon Sinek, British/American Author, Motivational Speaker & Marketing Consultant

[ii] John Maxwell, *Developing the Leader Within You 2.0*

[iii] Henri Frédéric Amiel (French: [amjɛl]; 27 September 1821 – 11 May 1881) was a Swiss moral philosopher, poet, and critic.

[iv] Marcus Tullius Cicero, Roman philosopher, statesman, lawyer, political theorist, and Roman constitutionalist. Cicero is widely considered one of Rome's greatest orators and prose stylists.

[v] Published on HBR.org, December 9, 2015

[vi] Bain & Company is a global management consultancy headquartered in Boston, Massachusetts. It is one of the 'Big Three' management consultancies (MBB).[7] The firm provides advice to public, private, and non-profit organizations.

[vii] Brendon Burchard is a #1 *New York Times* best-selling author and the world's leading High-Performance Coach

[viii] Marcus Anthony Lemonis (born November 16, 1973) is a Lebanese-born American businessman, investor, television personality, philanthropist and politician. He is currently the chairman and CEO of Camping World, Good Sam Enterprises, Gander Outdoors and The House Boardshop, in addition to being the star of *The Profit, a* CNBC reality show about saving small businesses.

[ix] August Turak is an award-winning author, speaker, consultant and contributor for Forbes.com and the BBC. Authored titles include *Business Secrets of the Trappist Monks* and Templeton Prize-Winning story, *Brother John.*

www.ingramcontent.com/pod-product-compliance
Lightning Source LLC
Chambersburg PA
CBHW021106210326
41598CB00016B/1349